CONTENTS

INTRODUCTION

The National Association for Stock Car Auto Racing, or NASCAR, is a popular motorsport in the United States. It is a special kind of racing that takes place on oval circuits and features drivers going fast around the track in stock cars. Even though the sport has experienced ups and downs throughout the years, millions of fans still tune in to watch each race.

Several important factors contribute to NASCAR's popularity. The sport is tremendously thrilling to watch. There is always a chance for a spectacular crash or a photo-finish when drivers are racing inches apart from one another at speeds of up to 200 miles per hour. Fans who are seeking an adrenaline rush are drawn to the game because of the high degree of excitement and unpredictability.

The tight relationship between NASCAR drivers and fans is another factor in the sport's success. NASCAR fans have the chance to get up close and personal with their favorite drivers, unlike followers of other sports who may only be able to see their favorite sportsmen from a distance. Many drivers engage with fans by signing autographs, posing for photos, and even attending fan events.

In addition to the thrill and accessibility, NASCAR has a strong cultural tie to America. Much of the sport's followers are from small towns and rural areas because it has its roots in the rural South. These communities frequently see NASCAR events as a way to unite and celebrate their mutual passion for racing.

Furthermore, the way NASCAR has adapted to the contemporary media landscape is another factor in the sport's popularity. Fans may now watch races from anywhere in the world and communicate with other fans online thanks to social media and streaming services. This has aided in extending the sport's appeal and attracting new followers from all around the world.

Many elements, such as the sport's excitement, accessibility, cultural relevance, and contemporary media presence, contribute to NASCAR's popularity. These factors have helped to create a devoted fan base that is passionate about the sport and invested in its continued success.

THE HISTORY OF NASCAR

The National Association for Stock Car Auto Racing, or NASCAR, has been in existence for more than 50 years. It is one of the quickest and most well-known motorsports in the world. It has a lengthy history that can be traced back to the 1920s and 1930s land speed record race. It also owes a lot to moonshine bootlegging, too.

- ## FOUNDATION

There was a period of time known as prohibition that forbade the sale and use of alcohol. This prompted people who created their own alcohol, known as bootleggers, to sell it on the illegal market. They needed to share their illegal alcohol with others, but they also needed to avoid getting caught by the police. They therefore required quick vehicles to convey their moonshine.

They were able to easily elude the authorities since they were able to combine diminutive stature with quick speed. Then, it became common to race these cars to see which one was the fastest. This developed into organized local and national races, and a technician by the name of William France Sr. eventually competed in one of the races at Daytona.

For fans of NASCAR, February 15, 1948, holds special significance because it was the day of the first official race held by the league. Red Byron was the inaugural NASCAR race winner, and the competition took place on a beach road course in Daytona Beach, Florida (11 years before the renowned Daytona International Speedway opened).

The Charlotte Fairgrounds Speedway in North Carolina hosted the group's first "Strictly Stock" competition the following year. The race is notable because it features the first female competitor in a NASCAR premier series race (Sara Christian finished 14th).

Throughout the following ten years, NASCAR racing's popularity grew steadily. The first Daytona 500 was watched by more than 41,000 spectators on February 22, 1959. By just two feet, Lee Petty (Richard Petty's father) was declared the winner in the photo-finish. The race, which is still conducted in February every year, is the most esteemed competition in NASCAR's calendar. Wendell Scott, competing at Jacksonville Speedway in December 1963, made history by being the first African-American to triumph in a major NASCAR race.

- ## NASCAR. (1972-1992)

Since the 1950s, the children of Bill France Sr. have worked for NASCAR (the organization remains a privately-owned family business to this day). Then in 1972, William France Sr. gave his son Bill France Jr. control of NASCAR. France Jr. had a key role in bringing NASCAR races out of the South and onto the national stage during his tenure as the organization's second president. Also, NASCAR started to expand internationally.

The Daytona 500 was the first big NASCAR race to be broadcast nationally live from start to finish thanks to a contract signed by France Jr. with CBS Sports in 1979. The timing couldn't have been better, since a huge snowstorm kept folks in the Northeast and Midwest at home (and watching TV). Richard Petty won the thrilling race, but not before Cale Yarborough and Donnie Allison collided in the closing laps.

Petty's record-breaking seventh NASCAR Cup Series championship includes this victory. Later, in 1984, Petty achieved his 200th and last victory at the Firecracker 400, setting a record that has not since been beaten.

Although Petty's success in this era was legendary, one of the most memorable events undoubtedly occurred in the 1992 season finale at Atlanta Motor Speedway during a so-called "passing of the torch." This is due to the fact that this event was both Jeff Gordon's inaugural race and the culmination of Richard Petty's illustrious career.

- ## AN ICON HAS DIED (1993-2001)

Clifford Allison, Davey Allison's younger brother, perished in a NASCAR Busch Series practice accident in 1992. When Davey Allison and Alan Kulwicki perished in separate accidents a year later, upsetting the NASCAR community, the calamity was further exacerbated.

Three drivers passed away in 1992, but things started to get better for NASCAR in 1994 with the start of the Brickyard 400 at the storied Indianapolis Motor Speedway, where Jeff Gordon won the 2.5-mile race just two days after turning 23. By winning at North Carolina's Rockingham Speedway later in the year, Dale Earnhardt Sr. tied Richard Petty's record for most championships by winning his seventh.

As race coverage spreads to Fox, NBC, and Turner Sports before the end of the decade, NASCAR keeps advancing into the mainstream. Yet after Dale Earnhardt Sr. died in a collision on the Daytona 500's penultimate lap at the storied Daytona International Speedway in February 2001, the NASCAR world once more came to a standstill. To help increase overall driver safety, rule revisions resulting from this tragic and horrific incident mandated the adoption of a HANS device by all NASCAR drivers.

To help increase general driver safety, this terrible and disturbing incident would lead to rule amendments requiring all NASCAR drivers to use neck-stabilizing equipment, known as a HANS device.

- ## A NEW AGE (2002-2016)

NASCAR opened its Research and Development Center in Concord, North Carolina, in 2003, partly as a result of Dale Earnhardt Sr passing. The state-of-the-art facility provides safety testing and performance engineering services to race teams and automakers. At the same time, Brian France, Bill Jr.'s son, takes over as NASCAR's president.

In 2004, the communications firm NEXTEL took over R.J. Reynolds' Winston cigarette brand's role as major sponsor. Also, NASCAR makes changes to the way championship points are calculated. The NASCAR Hall of Fame's initial class was announced in 2010. On-site awards are given to Richard Petty and Junior Johnson, while posthumous awards are given to Dale Earnhardt Sr., Bill France Sr., and Bill France Jr.

In addition to winning the rookie of the year award and becoming the first female to win an IndyCar Series race, Danica Patrick brings her IndyCar fame and success to NASCAR. She won the fan vote for best driver in 2012, and a year later made history by becoming the first female driver to ever take the pole position in the premier series.

With a record-breaking seventh victory in the premier series championship in 2016, Jimmie Johnson joins Richard Petty and Dale Earnhardt Sr. as the most successful drivers in NASCAR history. As the primary NASCAR sponsor, Monster Energy replaces Sprint/NEXTEL.

- ## NASCAR TODAY (2017-PRESENT)

From the timing of commercial TV breaks to the introduction of a playoff structure, NASCAR made a number of modifications. The major changes that have gone into effect since the beginning of the 2017 season are intended to keep spectators interested in every head-to-head match.

The following year, NASCAR purchased the Automobile Racing Club of America (ARCA), a stock car racing sanctioning body in the Midwest. ARCA has evolved over time into a launching pad for drivers looking to join NASCAR's premier series. Also, Jim France became NASCAR's president at this time, and Brian France resigned as the organization's leader. Jim is Bill France Jr.'s brother and Bill France Sr son.

Virtual racing, or eSports, have been a part of NASCAR history since 2010. Starting in 2018, the relationship with iRacing underwent significant improvements, including a stronger connection to the actual NASCAR series. The NASCAR Coca-Cola iRacing Series makes its debut in 2020 with a prize fund of $300,000 and broadcast coverage.

NASCAR was impacted by the COVD-19 epidemic in early 2020, just like all professional sports. Yet, quick action (such closing the stands to spectators and lowering the number of staff members present) allows NASCAR racing to resume competition in May before other sports. Homebound spectators swarm to the television race coverage and some semblance of routine.

The main reasons that racing has returned for 2022 are packed fans and a full schedule. In addition, NASCAR reinstates its qualifying system for every premier series race, which was abandoned over the previous two years due to the pandemic.

THE NASCAR SCHEDULE

Despite being a lengthy season with 38 races spread over 10 months, NASCAR does have a set schedule. Every year, the racing season begins in February and finishes in November. - It's incredible how little a 10-month, 36-race schedule (excluding the All-Star race and Bud Shootout) compares to what NASCAR drivers raced in the past. Drivers competed in 62 events in the 1964 Grand National Series, which is now known as the Sprint Cup Series, which interestingly enough ran from November 10, 1963 to November 8, 1964. That season sure is long. Naturally, things have changed, and the NASCAR series (as well as its schedule) have done the same.

The regular season schedules for each of NASCAR's three national series are different. Each racer competes on a variety of superspeedways, short tracks, intermediate tracks, and road courses during the season. These weekend activities take place across the United States and occasionally in Canada, from Florida to California.

Each series begins its regular season calendar in February at Daytona International Speedway, with the exception of scheduled exhibition races that do not count toward championship standings, which typically take place for the Cup Series during Daytona Speedweeks and the midseason All-Star Race.

NASCAR CUP SERIES REGULAR SEASON:

A total of 26 races (usually on Sundays) begins with the Daytona 500 in February. Throughout the season, there are various more "Crown Jewel" races. The All-Star Race takes place in the middle of the regular season. After 26 races, the regular-season champion is crowned and given 15 points. The NASCAR Cup Series Playoffs are open to the top 16 drivers.

The breakdown of each regular season is as follows:

- **SERIES CUP**

With 26 events on the regular season schedule, the Cup Series races most frequently on Sundays and kicks off each season of competition with the historic Daytona 500. The coveted "Crown Jewels," or contests that have historically been significant to the sport, are sprinkled throughout the schedule. The Coca-Cola 600 at Charlotte Motor Speedway, the Brickyard 400 at Indianapolis Motor Speedway, and the Southern 500 at Darlington Raceway also hold this distinction in addition to the Daytona 500.

The Coca-Cola 600, sometimes known as the Coke 600, is always the longest race on the calendar. The 600-mile marathon tests the drivers' endurance and the team's effectiveness. The length of almost every other oval race is between 300 and 500 miles. Drivers from the Cup Series race in the All-Star Race in the middle of the schedule for the chance to win a $1 million prize. Drivers who have either won a race this season or the season prior, previously won an All-

Star Race, or hold a Cup Series championship qualified to compete in this special showcase. If a driver doesn't meet these requirements, they have two options: enter the All-Star Open and race their way in through heats, or win the fan vote.

Drivers can advance to the NASCAR Playoffs with enough points or a win during the regular season by doing well in races.

A regular-season champion is recognized after the 26 races of the regular season and is given an additional 15 points for the playoffs. The playoffs are open to sixteen drivers.

• XFINITY SERIES

The Xfinity Series likewise has a 26-race schedule for its regular season, with races often taking place on Saturdays at the facility. With a few exceptions each year, the Xfinity Series competes at many of the same venues as the Cup Series, typically on the same weekend. It is occasionally possible for Cup Series drivers to participate in specific Xfinity events when they are present in order to get track time before the Sunday race.

The regular-season finale, playoffs, and some other races designated under the Dash 4 Cash midseason program are off-limits to Cup drivers who want to collect series points. Only five of the first 25 races on the Xfinity schedule are open to Cup drivers with three or more years of full-time experience in the premier series. Regulars of the Xfinity Series compete for cash prizes over a four-race span during the Dash 4 Cash races.

Drivers collect points for stage finishes and overall finishes throughout each race, just like in the premier series, enabling them to contend for playoff slots.

A regular-season champion is recognized after the 26 races of the regular season and is given an additional 15 points for the playoffs. The playoffs are advanced by twelve drivers.

• THE CAMPING WORLD TRUCK SERIES

The Camping World Truck Series, the third national series, runs each season on a lighter schedule than the top two, with a 15-race regular-season schedule that mostly consists of Friday night features. Performance rewards and incentives, like the Triple Truck Challenge, are scattered throughout these competitions, nevertheless. These competitions give Truck Series regulars the chance to compete for financial rewards at certain intervals throughout the season, similar to the Xfinity Series Dash 4 Cash.

Drivers from the Truck Series frequently compete against those from the Cup and Xfinity during the season. Drivers who are collecting championship points in the Xfinity Series and Cup Series are ineligible to earn points or race in the Triple Truck Challenge races or the season finale.. Only five of the first 14 races on the schedule allow Cup drivers with three or more seasons of full-time experience in the premier series to participate.

Following formatting convention, drivers receive points throughout the regular season for stage finishes and overall standings.

Following the completion of the 15 regular season races, a regular season winner is declared and given 15 extra points for the postseason. The playoffs will include ten drivers.

NASCAR TRACK TYPES

There Are Four Main Types Of NASCAR Tracks:

- Short Track,
- Intermediate Ovals,
- Superspeedways,
- Road Courses.

The majority of racetracks have an oval form and four distinct curves. Pit road, where racers must briefly leave the circuit in order to obtain mechanical tune-ups or have their cars supplied with gas, is one of the track's components. Grandstands, which are bleachers with a net protecting them from flying debris and can hold hundreds of thousands of spectators, are also located all around the track.

Small tracks typically have a length of under a mile. They are usually the most difficult to race on because they call for both control and speed. Bristol Motor Raceway in Tennessee and Martinsville Speedway in Ridgeway, Virginia are two notable short tracks in NASCAR.

Intermediate oval tracks, which are around 1.5 miles long, are great for racing in all situations. The Charlotte Motor Speedway in Concord, New Hampshire, and the Homestead-Miami Speedway in Homestead, Florida are two popular intermediate tracks on the NASCAR schedule.

The Superspeedway track is over two miles long. Daytona International Speedway in Daytona Beach, Florida, is the most well-known superspeedway. Longer races that take place on streets or specialized racetracks are called road courses. Road courses have winding curves and are not ovals. A well-known NASCAR road course is the Indianapolis Motor Speedway Road Course, which is situated in Speedway, Indiana, an Indianapolis suburb.

THE COMPOSITION OF NASCAR TRACKS

NASCAR circuits have slightly different natural surfaces. Asphalt is the most common material for tracks, and each one has a distinct roughness that can range from smooth to rough. Racers frequently prefer smoother tracks because they make it easier to maneuver the car, whereas rougher tracks are more challenging and need complicated maneuvers and a lot of gear shifting. Certain tracks, including Martinsville, Dover, and Bristol, employ concrete in their corners. Nashville Superspeedway is the first NASCAR course made entirely out of concrete.

• TRACK HISTORY IN NASCAR

Originally, NASCAR tracks were dirt ovals. Nearly all of them were paved over to become more indicative of the tracks that dominate the NASCAR schedule in the present day after it was realized that these types of tracks were not favorable to the more thrilling parts of racing, such as speed and steep corners.

Bristol Motor Speedway is a NASCAR short track track that was once known as Bristol International Raceway and Bristol Raceway. It is situated in Bristol, Tennessee. It was built in 1960, and on July 30, 1961, it hosted its first NASCAR race. Because to its unique characteristics, including its extremely steep banking mixed with its short length, its all-concrete surface, its two pit roads, and the stadium-style seating, Bristol is one of the most well-liked tracks on the NASCAR schedule.

The concrete track at Bristol Motor Raceway normally measures half a mile. The track is temporarily transformed into a dirt track for the Bristol dirt race by adding a layer of dirt to the surface.

23,000 cubic yards of dirt, or roughly 2,300 truckloads, are hauled in to prepare for the dirt race. The concrete track is then covered with the dirt to produce a track that is appropriate for dirt racing. A lot of planning and preparation go into the process of turning a concrete track to a dirt track.

The race was dubbed the Food City Dirt Race in 2021 as it was moved to a version of the track with a dirt surface.

• A NASCAR TRACK'S SHAPE

The shapes of NASCAR racetrack are extremely diverse. Regular ovals make up short tracks, while other regular and irregular oval shapes make up intermediate tracks. Superspeedways are big, conventional oval tracks with sharply banked bends. Road courses have a variety of straightaways, chicanes, and turns that are made in both directions.

• NASCAR TRACK DISTANCES

The length of the track indicates how far the car must drive during a race lap. The range of distances is from .25 miles to 4 miles. Shorter circuits like Bristol Motor Speedway (half a mile each lap) and intermediate tracks like the Daytona 500 (2.5 miles per lap) require competitors to successfully complete 500 laps, respectively. Sharper and trickier curves also tend to be found on shorter tracks.

• NASCAR PIT STOP

Pit road is an off-track location used for pit stops at every NASCAR track. Pit stops are an essential part of every race and need to be timed carefully in order to keep up with the opposition. When a vehicle needs petrol, new tires, or damage repair, the driver pulls over to the side of the track and parks it in the pit stall where a team of skilled mechanics swiftly fixes it before releasing it back onto the circuit. Due to the need for speed and accuracy when changing the race car, quick pit stops are frequently the difference between losing and winning a race. As a result, these stops are now high-pressure scenarios.

HOW MANY NASCAR RACE TRACKS EXIST?

The Cup Series features 26 different NASCAR race track. The Charlotte Roval and the Chariotte Motor Raceway oval are included in this total as separate tracks. A new track is added to the Xfinity Series, while three additional tracks not on the Cup Series calendar are added to the Truck Series. The top three national NASCAR series now have a total of 30 tracks. There are 42 NASCAR tracks across all divisions, along with a number of other tracks used in regional series.

CAR EVOLUTION OF NASCAR

- **GENERATION 1**

What is currently commonly accepted as Generation 1 made its debut with the governing body in 1948 and resembled its on-street counterparts almost perfectly. Several manufacturers, including Chevrolet, Chrysler, Volkswagen, and even Jaguar, participated in NASCAR.

There were three requirements: Each vehicle had to have a body and frame that were completely stock. This means that the body and structure of the car cannot be altered once the driver buys it from the dealer. It was to remain unchanged.

The NASCAR race vehicles of this generation were the only ones with real doors. The doors were a serious problem for driver safety because they were modified street cars. In the end, NASCAR required that the doors be bolted or welded shut, which gave rise to breaking in through the window.

Heavy-duty rear axles were the third and last allowed change, and they were used to stop rollovers. Nothing further could be done to the car outside the three aforementioned alterations. The Strictly Stock vehicles were in operation until NASCAR forced the Grand National Division to undergo its first significant competitive overhaul in 1966.

- **GENERATION 2**

NASCAR needs a new generation of vehicles to keep up with the new superspeedways that are being designed and built in 1967.

In contrast to prior years, when anything was allowed as long as it was stock, NASCAR sought greater parity with its new regulations package. While the "win on Sunday, sell on Monday" philosophy persisted, NASCAR let teams to be more lenient with frame alterations. The chassis may be modified by the teams, but the body had to stay stock. The cars had no doors but were otherwise very similar to their on-the-road counterparts. Richard Petty's 1973 Dodge Charger resembled a vehicle that a client might have purchased from a nearby Dodge dealer almost exactly.

For the construction and design of NASCAR's chassis, three businesses—Holman-Moody, Banjo Matthews, and Hutchensen-Pagan—were hired. As a result, NASCAR began to switch from stock vehicles to race cars with unique designs. When the 1980s arrived, this became even clearer.

- **GENERATION 3**

The days of an automobile being showroom to track had long since passed by 1981, as these custom-built vehicles only resembled their off-track equivalents in passing. The cars downsized, according to NASCAR, which was supposed to help with showroom equivalency, but they were still largely different.

The modifications increased the cars' speed and improved their aerodynamics. Once more, there were no doors to be seen, larger spoilers, a more streamlined design, manufacturer support from GM, Ford, and Chrysler, and teams had access to six distinct brands. Teams could still obtain body panels and other parts straight from manufacturers because to the three parent corporations' strong support.

The cars' wheelbases were 110 inches, a substantial decrease from prior models. This generation's lifespan was the shortest, lasting only one decade, and the 1990s saw the introduction of an entirely new game.

- **GENERATION 4**

NASCAR introduced the platform generation that is currently regarded as its most recognizable in 1991. These vehicles had entirely altered bodies and barely resembled their street-legal equivalents. Except for the hazy shape and markings, it was obvious that these were track-specific race automobiles rather than regular street cars.

Teams started using wind tunnels to optimize aerodynamics at this time as aero grip started to outperform its mechanical counterpart.

Steel bodies were gradually replaced by fiberglass in the bodies, which also underwent alteration. The car's weight was lowered as a result, increasing its weight-to-power ratio. Even while the components somewhat resembled the showroom models, many teams only used these characteristics for show. This covered the car's bumpers, front end, and rear end.

Three GM brands left the market during the Gen-4 era: Pontiac in 2004, Buick in 1992, and Oldsmobile in 1994. Dodge made a comeback in 2001, while Toyota made its entrance as the first Asian automaker in 2007. NASCAR rules still mandated that the showroom equivalents be produced in the country, with Toyota plants located in Kentucky, Texas, and California.

Although the Gen 4's final full-time season of competition was in 2006, it competed in 2007 with the controversial Car of Tomorrow, the vehicle from the following generation.

- **GENERATION 5**

Everything that came before The Car of Tomorrow was entirely different. The COT was a visual departure for the Cup Series, including a front splitter and a rear wing that was virtually V8 Supercar-like in design.

In the interest of competition, the splitter and wing could be changed, however, the splitter proved more agile when used on the infield grass. Throughout its existence, Chevy, Dodge, Ford, and Toyota all complained that the bodywork was all identical and had no manufacturer relevance at all.

Throughout the sport's history, this car did result in the biggest safety improvements. When Michael McDowell crashed in 2008 at Texas Motor Speedway, hitting the wall at almost 200 mph and barrel rolling down the straightaway, it was clear that the COT was a changeable tank of a platform. After ten rollovers, McDowell managed to escape unharmed. Its safety was further attested to by violent incidents involving Carl Edwards, Ryan Newman, Kyle Busch, and Kasey Kahne.

Halfway through 2010, the rear wing was replaced with a spoiler after receiving such negative fan feedback, and the splitter was shrunk in an effort to lessen the risk of terminal damage from even the slightest contact. After Brad Keselowski and Dodge won the 2012 championship,

Dodge left the competition since so few teams had committed to the Manufacturer for the Gen-6

era.

• GENERATION 6

The currently in use NASCAR vehicles' current generation was introduced by Chevrolet, Ford, and Toyota. The Gen 6 saw the comeback of manufacturer identity with customized bodywork that mirrored equivalents in showrooms. The chassis under the shell had very limited room for competitive maneuvering and was mostly built to specification.

These vehicles got bigger, quicker, and more durable as time went on, depending on maximum aerodynamic grip to maintain speed on all kinds of race tracks. During this time, the on-track action on some of the biggest courses suffered, but the real competition could be found in the shops. There had never been a more furious game of cat and mouse between the sanctioning body and the teams.

During this time, NASCAR frequently employed some of the top veteran crew chiefs to act as competition directors. Later, it developed a cutting-edge laser light inspection station to do what conventional templates were unable to do for the first decade of its existence.

This vehicle will be utilized through the 2021 season before being replaced in 2022 by the Next-Gen, a new generation of standard vehicle.

- **GENERATION 7**

The Next-Gen designation will be used to introduce the seventh generation of NASCAR Cup Series vehicles in 2022. There has never been a leap in evolution like the one under the next platform, despite the fact that every generation of car represented an improvement in technology, safety, or aesthetics in some noticeable way.

For the first time ever, Cup Series vehicles will be mostly built to specification, requiring teams to buy parts and accessories from authorized vendors rather than the open market or their own shops. Rather of being designed, cars will primarily become kits that must be assembled. This has been done to maintain competitive parity and control costs.

Only the inside engine and outside body will vary from one car to the next. Since NASCAR ceased using production vehicles in the 1980s, Chevrolet, Ford, and Toyota have all developed unique body designs that are the closest portrayal of stock cars.

The platform will initially employ the ICE V8 engine formula of the present generation, but over the course of the following ten years, an electric or hybrid counterpart will be adopted.

In that it ultimately modernizes regulations that had been in place since the 1960s, the automobile is evolutionary. The Next-Gen will have a center-lock lug nut, independent rear suspension, 18-inch wheels, and low-profile tires. It uses a transaxle with a five-speed sequential transmission (plus reverse). The greenhouse is a reflection of its equivalents in the showroom. The entire package has been created to encourage more OEMs to join Chevrolet, Ford, and Toyota, and the platform has been created to support a wide range of manufacturers. This lowers the entry bar, bridges the competitive gap between the mega teams and those who typically play in the middle of the field or worse, and bridges the competitive gap between the two groups of teams.

NASCAR PAST CHAMPIONS

Many champions have been crowned by NASCAR over the years in a variety of racing series and levels of competition. The previous winners of the premier NASCAR Cup Series are listed below:

1. 1949: Red Byron
2. 1950: Bill Rexford
3. 1951: Herb Thomas
4. 1952: Tim Flock
5. 1953: Herb Thomas
6. 1954: Lee Petty
7. 1955: Tim Flock
8. 1956: Buck Baker
9. 1957: Buck Baker
10. 1958: Lee Petty
11. 1959: Lee Petty
12. 1960: Rex White
13. 1961: Ned Jarrett
14. 1962: Joe Weatherly
15. 1963: Joe Weatherly
16. 1964: Richard Petty
17. 1965: Ned Jarrett
18. 1966: David Pearson
19. 1967: Richard Petty
20. 1968: David Pearson
21. 1969: David Pearson
22. 1970: Bobby Isaac
23. 1971: Richard Petty
24. 1972: Richard Petty
25. 1973: Benny Parsons
26. 1974: Richard Petty
27. 1975: Richard Petty
28. 1976: Cale Yarborough
29. 1977: Cale Yarborough
30. 1978: Cale Yarborough
31. 1979: Richard Petty
32. 1980: Dale Earnhardt Sr.
33. 1981: Darrell Waltrip
34. 1982: Darrell Waltrip
35. 1983: Bobby Allison

36   1984: Terry Labonte
37   1985: Darrell Waltrip
38   1986: Dale Earnhardt Sr.
39   1987: Dale Earnhardt Sr.
40   1988: Bill Elliott
41   1989: Rusty Wallace
42   1990: Dale Earnhardt Sr.
43   1991: Dale Earnhardt Sr.
44   1992: Alan Kulwicki
45   1993: Dale Earnhardt Sr.
46   1994: Dale Earnhardt Sr.
47   1995: Jeff Gordon
48   1996: Terry Labonte
49   1997: Jeff Gordon
50   1998: Jeff Gordon
51   1999: Dale Jarrett
52   2000: Bobby Labonte
53   2001: Jeff Gordon
54   2002: Tony Stewart
55   2003: Matt Kenseth
56   2004: Kurt Busch
57   2005: Tony Stewart
58   2006: Jimmie Johnson
59   2007: Jimmie Johnson
60   2008: Jimmie Johnson
61   2009: Jimmie Johnson
62   2010: Jimmie Johnson
63   2011: Tony Stewart
64   2012: Brad Keselowski
65   2013: Jimmie Johnson
66   2014: Kevin Harvick
67   2015: Kyle Busch
68   2016: Jimmie Johnson
69   2017: Martin Truex Jr.
70   2018: Joey Logano
71   2019: Kyle Busch
72   2020: Chase Elliott
73   2021: Kyle Larson
74   2022: Joey Logano

As previous winners of the sport's top series, these drivers have permanently inscribed their names in NASCAR history. Drivers engage in a taxing 36-race schedule every year in an effort to win the NASCAR Cup Series championship.

NASCAR RULES AND REGULATIONS

NASCAR races are thrilling to watch because of the fast-paced action, fierce competition, and emphasis on safety. Behind the scenes, NASCAR racing is governed by a large set of laws and rules. These regulations guarantee the sport's fairness, security, and consistency. We will look at a few of the several laws and ordinances that control NASCAR racing in this e-book.

- ## CAR SPECIFICATIONS

Car specs are one of the most significant regulations in NASCAR racing. NASCAR has strict rules governing the types of vehicles that can participate in its competitions. The maximum weight and horsepower for automobiles are 3,400 pounds and 750, respectively. Also, they must have a roll cage, a fire extinguisher, and window netting among other safety features.

The height, width, size of the spoiler, and size of the fuel cell are just a few of the dimensions and shapes that are governed by NASCAR. These rules are in place to make sure that all cars are constructed in accordance with the same standards and that no team has an unfair advantage.

- ## RACE FORMAT

There are several different racing forms used by NASCAR, including oval, road course, and dirt tracks. Each race has a distinct format that is controlled by NASCAR rules. For instance, races can be played in stages with pit stops only permitted at predetermined race breaks. Also, NASCAR has regulations regarding the number of laps and vehicles that may compete in a given race.

- ## PENALTIES

Regarding driver behaviour and sportsmanship, NASCAR has tight guidelines. NASCAR authorities have the right to fine drivers who drive recklessly or dangerously. Fines, point deductions, or even a suspension from racing are all possible penalties.

NASCAR has additional regulations for pit road behavior, such as speed limitations and the number of crew members that can cross the wall during pit stops. Penalties and even disqualification from the race may follow violations of these rules.

Penalties and even disqualification from the race may follow violations of these rules.

- **SAFETY**

In NASCAR racing, safety is of the utmost importance. Safety gear, like as helmets, fire suits, and HANS devices, is subject to NASCAR regulations. In addition, NASCAR has track safety regulations that include the usage of SAFER barriers and caution flags during competitions.

A medical crew from NASCAR is also present at every race to offer immediate care in the case of an accident. Before being permitted to return to the track, drivers who have been in accidents must pass a medical evaluation.

- **TESTING**

Driver and team testing is subject to NASCAR regulations. To prevent teams from getting an unfair advantage, NASCAR limits the number of tests that teams can run annually. In addition, NASCAR sets guidelines on the kinds of testing that are permitted, including track testing and testing in a wind tunnel.

- **POINTS SYSTEM**

The victor of the championship is decided by the NASCAR points system at the end of the season. Points are awarded to drivers according to how they place in each race. At the end of the season, the driver with the most points is crowned champion.

Additionally, NASCAR has regulations governing how bonus points are awarded, such as for winning stages or leading the most laps. These extra points have a significant impact on the final rankings and have the potential to determine the winner of the championship.

- **TECHNIQUES CHECKS**

Before and after each race, NASCAR performs technical inspections on the vehicles. These examinations guarantee that all vehicles adhere to the rules established by NASCAR. Vehicles that don't pass inspection risk being fined or perhaps eliminated from the competition.

- **DRIVER AND CAR CHANGES**

From the start of the first practice session until the finish of the race, teams are required to employ a single car. Teams may switch to a backup car if one of their cars crashes during practice or qualifying, but if they race a different vehicle than the one that passes the initial inspection, that vehicle must start at the back of the pack.

During a race weekend, engine and transmission changes are not permitted. Except for restrictor plate races, Xfinity and Truck Series engines must last for two race weekends. Teams competing in the Cup Series are limited to using a maximum of 23 engines over the course of the season (13 engines must last at least two race weekends). If either is changed, the player will start at the back of the field. At Pocono Raceway, transmission changes are permitted both on race weekends and road course weekends.

Changes in the driver are allowed, but if the car starts the race with a different driver than the one who qualified it, the car will start at the back of the pack. It is also acceptable for teams to switch drivers during the race while making pit stops, however any positional penalties incurred must be paid by the team. All of the points, statistics, and prize money are awarded to the driver who starts the race.

FLAGS

Flags Like the majority of other sanctioning organizations, NASCAR will use flags to warn the drivers of the track's conditions. Although NASCAR is a member club of ACCUS, the U.S. motor racing sporting organization and representative to the FIA World Motor Sport Council, NASCAR does not follow the FIA standards and does not employ the flag system described in the FIA International Sporting Code. The white flag, which is used in NASCAR and other North American championships to indicate that the leader is on the final lap, is used to indicate the presence of a slower car in FIA ISC-regulated competitions like Formula One and the majority of European championships. Moreover, the FIA ISC's blue flag does not have a diagonal stripe, and a driver is penalized when it is black.

WHAT DOES EACH OF THE NASCAR FLAGS MEAN?

- ### BLACK FLAG

The black flag is intended to draw attention to an individual driver who has broken the law or who has severe damage that needs to be repaired right away. According to NASCAR's official rules and regulations, a driver who receives the black flag is required to leave the track immediately and head to their pit box so that the vehicle may be rapidly serviced or fixed.

Once the repairs have been authorized by a race official, they will be permitted to resume the race.

- ### BLUE FLAG

Only at road courses is the blue flag displayed, indicating that there are problems farther down the track that are difficult to perceive. The Blue flag just indicates that drivers should exercise caution and does not necessarily indicate that the weather is poor.

- ### BLUE FLAG WITH DIAGONAL YELLOW STRIPE

Drivers are warned when they notice the blue-striped flag that a quicker vehicle is coming to pass them. The flag signals that the driver being passed must slow down or move out of the way so that the race leaders can pass them. The flag is only raised when the quicker car is ahead by at least a complete lap (a full circuit around the track).

- ### CHECKERED FLAG

The race is declared over when the checkered flag is raised. The race is over when the driver crosses the finish line.

- ### GREEN FLAG

The green flag signals the beginning of a race, stage, or a restart following a caution. As soon as the green flag is raised, the driver in first place picks up speed and the field begin to roll.

• GREEN AND WHITE CHECKERED FLAG

The flagman will wave a checkered green and white flag to signal an overtime restart once the safety problem has been resolved because a race cannot terminate on a caution during the final laps. The race will restart normally after the checkered green and white flag appears, for instance, if a collision occurs on the second-to-last lap and drivers are required to follow the safety car. In this case, two overtime laps will be added.

• RED FLAG

When officials become aware of poor weather and hazardous track conditions, the red flag is raised. Drivers are required to head back to the pit lane until it is safe to resume racing rather than following a safety car and slowing down.

• BLACK AND RED FLAGS

When both the red and black flags are raised simultaneously, practice or qualifying is over. Drivers must slow down and head back to their garages when these two flags are raised, signaling the end of the practice session and their last chance to record a lap time.

• RED FLAG WITH YELLOW STRIPE

The pit lane is closed when a red flag with a yellow stripe is displayed. Every time the pack needs to be reformed, such as after a caution flag has been raised for an accident on the circuit, the pit lane is nearby.

• YELLOW FLAG

The yellow flag is used to alert drivers to potential track hazards, such as fluids, debris, significant collisions, or bad weather. Drivers are required to slow down and line up behind the pace car (a specially marked vehicle operated by a safety officer to set the speed when a safety concern develops) in order to follow the yellow flag until it stops waving, indicating that the hazard has been cleared.

OVERVIEW OF NASCAR CHAMPIONSHIP FROM 2015-2022

OVERVIEW OF THE NASCAR 2015 SEASON

The 2015 NASCAR season marked the 67th year of competitive stock car racing in the United States and the 44th year of the NASCAR Cup Series. The Sprint Unlimited demonstration race on February 14 marked the start of the season, which concluded with the Ford EcoBoost 400 on November 22.

The 2015 season saw a number of noteworthy changes. Most notably, NASCAR adopted a new set of regulations designed to increase safety and lessen track accidents. These regulations included a new qualifying procedure as well as modifications to the aerodynamics of the car.

Several new drivers made their debuts during the 2015 campaign, among them include the 2014 NASCAR Xfinity Series champion Chase Elliott.

The Daytona 500, the Brickyard 400, and the Southern 500 were among the 36 Cup Series events that took place throughout the season at various circuits throughout the United States. Joey Logano's victory in the Daytona 500, Kurt Busch's contentious suspension, and Jeff Gordon's farewell tour as he announced his retirement from full-time racing at the end of the season were some of the season's high points.

Four drivers remained in the race for the championship: Martin Truex Jr., Jeff Gordon, Kyle Busch, and Kevin Harvick. In 2014, Harvick claimed the title, making it his first NASCAR Cup Series victory.

For fans and the racing world, the 2015 NASCAR season was overall exciting and unforgettable. The 2015 season was a showcase for the innovation and excitement that made NASCAR such a popular sport, with new drivers, rule revisions, and fierce rivalry on the track.

Teams Who Participated In The 2015 NASCAR Season

The 2015 NASCAR season featured 42 teams, each of which entered one or more cars in the Cup Series. The following teams participated in the 2015 season:

- Jamie McMurray - Chip Ganassi Racing
- Brad Keselowski - Team Penske
- Joey Logano - Team Penske
- Kevin Harvick - Stewart-Haas Racing
- Jimmie Johnson - Hendrick Motorsports
- Dale Earnhardt Jr. - Hendrick Motorsports
- Matt Kenseth - Joe Gibbs Racing
- Denny Hamlin - Joe Gibbs Racing
- Jeff Gordon - Hendrick Motorsports

- Kurt Busch - Stewart-Haas Racing
- Carl Edwards - Joe Gibbs Racing
- Martin Truex Jr. - Furniture Row Racing
- Ryan Newman - Richard Childress Racing
- Kyle Busch - Joe Gibbs Racing
- Paul Menard - Richard Childress Racing
- Clint Bowyer - Michael Waltrip Racing
- Kasey Kahne - Hendrick Motorsports
- Aric Almirola - Richard Petty Motorsports
- Greg Biffle - Roush Fenway Racing
- Austin Dillon - Richard Childress Racing
- Casey Mears - Germain Racing
- Ricky Stenhouse Jr. - Roush Fenway Racing
- Danica Patrick - Stewart-Haas Racing
- David Ragan - Front Row Motorsports
- AJ Allmendinger - JTG Daugherty Racing
- Justin Allgaier - HScott Motorsports
- Trevor Bayne - Roush Fenway Racing
- Sam Hornish Jr. - Richard Petty Motorsports
- Cole Whitt - Front Row Motorsports
- Michael Annett - HScott Motorsports
- David Gilliland - Front Row Motorsports
- Brett Moffitt - Michael Waltrip Racing
- Alex Bowman - BK Racing
- Josh Wise - Phil Parsons Racing
- Jeb Burton - BK Racing
- Matt DiBenedetto - BK Racing
- Landon Cassill - Hillman-Circle Sport LLC
- Mike Bliss - Premium Motorsports
- JJ Yeley - BK Racing
- Timmy Hill - Premium Motorsports
- Travis Kvapil - The Motorsports Group
- Michael McDowell - Leavine Family Racing
- Bobby Labonte - Go FAS Racing

Throughout the 2015 NASCAR Cup Series season, each of these teams participated, with some fielding several drivers. This season was thrilling and competitive for both spectators and drivers because all of these teams were battling for the championship.

WINNER OF THE 2015 SPRINT CUP SERIES CHAMPIONSHIP.

In the last race of the 2015 NASCAR season on Sunday at Homestead-Miami Speedway, Kyle Busch defeated Kevin Harvick, Jeff Gordon, and Martin Truex Jr. to claim the Sprint Cup championship.

The winner of the Chase for the Sprint Cup would be determined by who of the final four title challengers finished in first place. In order to overtake Harvick and win the race and the championship, Busch exploited a late restart to take the lead away from Brad Keselowski.

Busch's triumph in the 2015 season was the result of years of toil and commitment. Although he had placed in the top five in the standings each of the previous four seasons, he had never been able to secure the championship. But for the driver of the #18 Toyota, everything came together in 2015.

But Busch's journey wasn't without its challenges. In actuality, he had a nightmare to begin the season. He was engaged in a terrible incident at the Xfinity Series race at Daytona in February that left him with a damaged right leg and left foot. Many people believed that his season had already ended before it had even started.

Busch was determined not to let his injury slow him down, though. He put forth a lot of effort with the help of his medical professionals and physical therapists to recover as quickly as possible, and by the time the Cup Series arrived in Indianapolis in late July, he was prepared to compete once more.

Busch's comeback was extraordinary in every way. In the regular season, he won five races, including a thrilling triumph at Sonoma Raceway in June where he overtook Jimmie Johnson on the last lap to claim the victory. Yet, his performance off the track was as excellent. It was the manner in which he conducted himself throughout the season, displaying a degree of tenacity and fortitude that motivated both his supporters and other rivals.

Busch was one of the leading contenders for the championship as the playoffs got underway. He won the opening race of the Round of 12 at Charlotte after winning the second race of the Round of 16 at New Hampshire. But what really solidified his position as the favorite for the title was his performance in the Round of 8's concluding race in Phoenix.

Busch won that race after dominating from start to finish, leading 118 of the 219 laps. It was a victory that made a statement, alerting the other competitors that Kyle Busch was the one to defeat and shocking the garage area.

Busch was once again the favorite for the Homestead-Miami Speedway championship race, but he had to contend with Kevin Harvick, Jeff Gordon, and Martin Truex Jr. Busch, though, refused to be frightened and turned in one of his career's most crucial performances.

He held off Harvick's late surge to grab the checkered flag and win his first Cup Series championship. He led a race-high 41 laps. He will never forget that, and it solidified his reputation as one of the greatest drivers of his generation.

Nevertheless, Busch's success wasn't only a personal victory for him. It was a victory for Joe Gibbs Racing as a whole and for all the supporters who had stuck by him through thick and thin. It served as a reminder that anything is possible if you believe in yourself and never give up. It was a testament to the effectiveness of hard effort, perseverance, and drive.

Busch has been one of NASCAR's best drivers in the years after his exceptional season, taking first place finishes in races and challenging for titles every year. No matter what he does in the future, he will always be known as the 2015 season's champion—a driver who overcame enormous obstacles to win the sport's highest honor.

WINNER OF THE 2015 NASCAR Xfinity SERIES

Many outstanding drivers engaged in fierce competition for the championship in the 2015 NASCAR Xfinity Series season. Yet Chris Buescher, who raced for Roush Fenway Racing, was declared the Xfinity Series' 2015 champion. Let's examine Buescher's championship-winning season in more detail.

In the season-opening race at Daytona International Speedway, where he placed third, Buescher made a strong start to his 2015 Xfinity Series campaign. In Atlanta Motor Speedway, he followed that up with another top-five performance, and by the time the championship race was the fourth one of the seasons, Buescher had assumed the lead.

Buescher showed incredible consistency throughout the season, frequently placing in the top 10 in races and being in the running for the championship. In Iowa Speedway in May, where he won the race after dominating it and leading 95 of the 250 laps, he earned his first victory of the year.

At Dover International Speedway in October, Buescher earned his second victory of the year after taking the lead on a late restart and holding off a charging Kyle Busch to win.

Buescher's two victories were unquestionably noteworthy, but it was his consistency over the course of the season that allowed him to win the championship. Throughout the course of the season, he finished with a total of 20 top-10 finishes and 11 top-five finishes, an amazing performance that allowed him to take the lead in the championship standings.

Buescher's impressive performances on the intermediate tracks were one of the factors that contributed to his success in the 2015 campaign. On the 1.5-mile ovals, he finished in the top five six times, including the runner-up position at Kentucky Speedway in September.

Aside from being the first Xfinity Series championship for Roush Fenway Racing since 2011, Buescher's victory was also significant because it was his first championship triumph in any NASCAR series.

Buescher was promoted to the Cup Series for the 2016 season after his productive Xfinity Series campaign in 2015, where he competed for Front Row Motorsports. Although he had trouble finding success in the Cup Series, he will always be recognized for his championship-winning season in the Xfinity Series.

Chris Buescher's championship-winning Xfinity Series season in 2015 was evidence of his prowess and dependability as a driver. His two victories, together with his remarkable track record of top-five and top-10 finishes, made him a worthy champion and solidified his place among NASCAR's up-and-coming drivers.

- ## THE 2015 NASCAR SEASON'S BEST RACE

The drama, the result, and the emotion that the autumn Martinsville race evoked outweighed the unsightly act that took place, despite the fact that it contained a moment that gave the impression that one was watching professional wrestling. Because it was one of the more well-known triumphs in NASCAR history when Gordon crossed the finish line for the 93rd time in his career. The fact that it earned him an improbable position in the championship final added to the grandeur, which wasn't missed on the champion, who celebrated by repeatedly displaying unrestrained passion and bouncing up and down like a child on Christmas morning.

Other notable races include the CampingWorld.com 500, the STP 500 in Martinsville, the Food City 500 in Bristol, the Quaker State 400 in Kentucky, the Daytona 500, and the STP 500 in Martinsville (Talladega).

- ## NASCAR'S WORST RACE OF THE 2015 CAMPAIGN

There are regrettably plenty of possibilities for this category because of a set of rules that essentially prevented side-by-side racing. Nonetheless, the scandal that occurred during Michigan's August race cannot be topped despite the wrench of uninteresting occurrences.

NASCAR management chose to use Michigan's second race as a glorified 400-mile test in the hopes that the introduction of a high-drag regulations package would increase excitement and produce more passing opportunities. That fell flat. Badly. Drivers found it difficult to overtake one another, the field quickly grew disorganized during restarts, and the winner (Kenseth) led 73 percent of the laps.

If there was any good news, it was the definitive debunking of the notion that the events at Daytona and Talladega might be repeated elsewhere.

OVERVIEW OF THE NASCAR 2016 SEASON

The 2016 NASCAR Sprint Cup Series marked the 45th Cup series season in the modern era and the 68th season of American professional stock car racing. The Sprint Unlimited, Can-Am Duel, and Daytona 500 marked the start of the season at Daytona International Speedway. The Ford EcoBoost 400 at Homestead-Miami Speedway marked the end of the season. Hendrick Motorsports' Jimmie Johnson earned his seventh drivers' title, tying Dale Earnhardt and Richard Petty for the most all-time. Becoming the first manufacturer to do so since Chevrolet last won the title in 2002, Toyota won the manufacturer's championship.

A new charter system that assured a starting position for 36 teams, the return of NASCAR's traditional group qualifying format, and the introduction of a new downforce package that decreased the cars' aerodynamic grip and increased passing opportunities were just a few of the significant changes that the NASCAR Cup Series underwent in 2016.

In addition, there were a number of significant retirements during the season, including three-time Cup Series champion Tony Stewart, who gave up full-time racing at the conclusion of the campaign. Jeff Gordon also played his last full-time season in 2016 after declaring his retirement the year before.

The Daytona 500, the Coca-Cola 600, and the Brickyard 400 were just a few of the 36 Cup Series events that took place throughout the season at various circuits throughout the United States. Two drivers, Kyle Busch of Joe Gibbs Racing and Jimmie Johnson of Hendrick Motorsports, dominated the season.

Some noteworthy events from the 2016 season were Carl Edwards' contentious decision to block Joey Logano in the final lap of the season-ending race at Homestead-Miami Speedway and Denny Hamlin's exciting victory at the Daytona 500. Tony Stewart also had an emotional victory at Sonoma Raceway.

A number of new drivers made their debuts during the 2016 season, including Chris Buescher, who triumphed at the Pocono Raceway rain-shortened race, and Chase Elliott, who took Jeff Gordon's place at Hendrick Motorsports.

For fans and the racing world, the 2016 NASCAR season was overall exciting and unforgettable. The 2016 season served as a testament to the excitement and creativity that make NASCAR such a cherished sport, with major rule changes, the retirement of iconic drivers, and tough racing on the track.

- **TEAMS THAT COMPETED IN THE 2016 NASCAR SEASON**

There were 40 teams in the 2016 NASCAR Sprint Cup Series, and they all participated in different events throughout the season. The following teams participated in the 2016 season:

- Jimmie Johnson - Hendrick Motorsports
- Kyle Busch - Joe Gibbs Racing
- Joey Logano - Team Penske
- Carl Edwards - Joe Gibbs Racing
- Matt Kenseth - Joe Gibbs Racing
- Kevin Harvick - Stewart-Haas Racing
- Kurt Busch - Stewart-Haas Racing
- Denny Hamlin - Joe Gibbs Racing
- Martin Truex Jr. - Furniture Row Racing
- Brad Keselowski - Team Penske
- Chase Elliott - Hendrick Motorsports
- Austin Dillon - Richard Childress Racing
- Jamie McMurray - Chip Ganassi Racing
- Ryan Newman - Richard Childress Racing
- Kasey Kahne - Hendrick Motorsports
- Kyle Larson - Chip Ganassi Racing
- Tony Stewart - Stewart-Haas Racing
- Chris Buescher - Front Row Motorsports
- Clint Bowyer - HScott Motorsports
- Greg Biffle - Roush Fenway Racing
- Paul Menard - Richard Childress Racing
- AJ Allmendinger - JTG Daugherty Racing
- Danica Patrick - Stewart-Haas Racing
- Casey Mears - Germain Racing
- Ricky Stenhouse Jr. - Roush Fenway Racing
- Brian Scott - Richard Petty Motorsports
- Trevor Bayne - Roush Fenway Racing
- Regan Smith - Tommy Baldwin Racing
- Michael McDowell - Leavine Family Racing
- David Ragan - BK Racing
- Matt DiBenedetto - BK Racing
- Jeffrey Earnhardt - Go FAS Racing
- Landon Cassill - Front Row Motorsports
- Reed Sorenson - Premium Motorsports

- Michael Annett - HScott Motorsports
- Bobby Labonte - Go FAS Racing
- Josh Wise - The Motorsports Group
- Cole Whitt - TriStar Motorsports
- Ty Dillon - Circle Sport - Leavine Family Racing
- Ryan Blaney - Wood Brothers Racing
- Dylan Lupton - BK Racing
- Patrick Carpentier - Go FAS Racing
- Alex Bowman - Tommy Baldwin Racing

Throughout the season, these teams fielded a total of 41 cars, with each team typically fielding one to four vehicles. The season began on February 21, 2016, at the Daytona International Speedway, and ended on November 20, 2016, at the Homestead-Miami Speedway, with a total of 36 races in which the drivers and teams competed.

WINNER OF THE 2016 SPRINT CUP SERIES CHAMPIONSHIP.

The 2016 NASCAR Sprint Cup Series marked the 45th Cup series season in the modern era and the 68th season of American professional stock car racing. The Sprint Unlimited, Can-Am Duel, and Daytona 500 marked the start of the season at Daytona International Speedway. The Ford EcoBoost 400 at Homestead-Miami Speedway marked the end of the season.

By overtaking Kyle Larson on the restart of the Ford EcoBoost 400, the season's penultimate race, on Sunday at Homestead-Miami Speedway, Jimmie Johnson won his seventh NASCAR Sprint Cup title.

Johnson is one of just three drivers with seven NASCAR championships, along with Richard Petty and Dale Earnhardt. Johnson's quest for a record-tying seventh Sprint Cup championship got off to a rocky start when NASCAR officials determined that his Hendrick Motorsports crew had made "unapproved adjustments" to the No. 48 car after it had already passed initial inspection. Johnson had to give up his 14th starting spot and line up 40th instead.

After the green flag was raised, Johnson didn't waste any time moving to the front. He gained 16 spots in just eight circuits, and by lap 15, he had returned to his original starting position. Johnson stayed close to the front and took advantage of the situation when it presented itself.

After Edwards and Logano collided after a restart with 10 laps remaining, the race was stopped for more than 30 minutes, ending Edwards' chances of winning the championship. Logano slammed into Edwards' rear as he attempted to block him, sending him against the interior wall. In the collision, Martin Truex Jr.'s vehicle also took fire, causing a delay while the first and second turns were cleaned up.

On the ensuing restart, Johnson moved up into second place behind Larson, however a last caution allowed Johnson the chance to not only win the championship but also the race. With two circuits remaining, he overtook Larson on the restart and created enough separation from the field to win by almost a half-second.

WINNER OF THE 2016 Xfinity SERIES

The 2016 NASCAR Xfinity Series is the 35th season of the American stock car racing series, which is sanctioned by NASCAR. The season began on February 20 at Daytona International Speedway and ended on November 19 at Homestead-Miami Speedway. The championship was won by Daniel Suárez of Joe Gibbs Racing, making him the first non-American to do so in NASCAR's top three divisions.

Suarez's triumph in the 2016 campaign was significant since it was the debut of a Mexican-born driver to a major NASCAR title. Yet more than just his ancestry contributed to the significance of his victory. He distinguished himself from his competitors by consistently outperforming the opposition and displaying a high level of talent and tenacity.

Suarez had a successful start to the year, taking home his first-ever Xfinity Series victory at Michigan in June. He continued on after that with another victory at Dover in October, and in 33 races overall, he concluded the regular season with 27 top-10 results. He qualified for the playoffs and became the favorite to win the championship thanks to a strong performance.

Allgaier, Sadler, and Jones were some of the challenging opponents Suarez had to deal with. But he maintained his composure, stuck to his course of action, and gave every lap his all. And as the final buzzer sounded, he had accomplished enough to seal the victory.

Suarez, his squad, and his supporters, who had seen him develop and mature during the season, were filled with genuine joy at the moment. Suarez's victory marked a significant advancement for diversity and inclusion in the sport, therefore it was also a significant occasion for NASCAR as a whole.

OVERVIEW OF THE NASCAR 2017 SEASON

The 2017 Monster Energy NASCAR Cup Series is the 46th Cup series season in the contemporary era and the 69th season of American professional stock car racing overall. The season began with its largest race, as NASCAR does in a way that is special every year. Several drivers dropped out of contention during the thrilling final few laps of the Daytona 500, and Kurt Busch emerged victorious for Stewart-Haas Racing to guarantee his immediate entry into the playoffs. Brad Keselowski would secure his place at the following race in Atlanta, and Martin Truex Jr. would join him by winning in Vegas a week later.

Since winning his record-tying seventh Cup championship, which he shares with Richard Petty and Dale Earnhardt, Jimmie Johnson entered the season as the defending champion. First-time series champion Martin Truex Jr. of Furniture Row Racing took home the trophy. The Manufacturers' Championship was won by Toyota for the second consecutive year.

A lot of drivers scored some unexpected victories in 2017 season. Under this structure, victories qualify you for the championship playoffs. One of the first underdogs to reach victory lane was Ryan Newman, who took Phoenix on a last-lap restart. The following few races would return to normal, with Kyle Larson and Jimmie Johnson taking home their first victories of the year. At Richmond, Joey Logano would also succeed in winning a race, but his victory would be overturned by a post-race technical review. In the end, Joey would pay a steep price for this.

Ricky Stenhouse Jr., Austin Dillon, and Ryan Blaney all picked up their first victories at the midpoint of the season to lock up their berths in the championship playoffs. As the series progressed toward the championship playoffs, it became clear that certain prominent drivers would be left out as Kyle Busch, Kevin Harvick, Denny Hamlin, and even Kasey Kahne reached victory lane.

With six races remaining before the cutoff, thirteen drivers had claimed victories, leaving only sixteen drivers qualified to move on to the ten-race playoffs. This resulted in a competitive race for the final three positions, with Clint Bowyer, Jamie McMurray, Chase Elliott, and Matt Kenseth competing against the typical front-runners, Chase Elliott, Erik Jones, and Daniel Suarez. After all was said and done, none of the seven drivers would take home a victory, but Elliott, Kenseth, and McMurray would capture the top three positions in terms of points.

The sixteen candidates had been chosen, leaving ten races for the championship. Truex Jr. entered the ten-race shootout with a significant edge over his competitors thanks to the addition of stage racing and playoff points. This was because of the number of race wins and stage wins he had amassed over the season. He demonstrated his ability for a championship by winning the first playoff race at Chicagoland, which would ensure him a place in the following round of three races and prevent him from being subject to the first elimination.

When a late-race pass denied Chase Elliott his first race victory, Kyle Busch, who many believed to be Truex's biggest contender for the championship, would earn the second win of the playoffs in New Hampshire and then go back-to-back by winning at Dover. Ryan Newman, Austin Dillon, Kasey Kahne, and Kurt Busch would be the first four drivers out after the first three rounds of the playoffs, reducing the field of competitors from sixteen to twelve.

Truex would begin the second round of the playoffs at Charlotte with his sixth victory of the year, securing him a place in the next round once more. Many rightly foresaw that the following race, which was held in Talladega, may have significant title ramifications. Before retiring, Dale Earnhardt Jr. would win the pole position, but Brad Keselowski would win the race.

Numerous championship candidates, including Kyle Busch, Kyle Larson, and other drivers, departed Alabama in a precarious position for the upcoming elimination race in Kansas. Despite being guaranteed a spot in the next round, Truex would take home the win for a record-tying eighth time, with Kyle Busch barely holding on to beat Kyle Larson, who would join Ricky Stenhouse Jr., Matt Kenseth, and Jamie McMurray in being knocked out.

All three of NASCAR's national series' race formats and scoring structures underwent significant alterations for the 2017 season, which were revealed on January 23 during a press conference. The majority of races include three stages, with the first two often covering about a quarter of the total distance and the third stage typically covering half of it. The Coca-Cola 600, which is divided into four 100-lap stages, is the sole exception to the points race rule. A race can be stopped with a winner during the third stage due to circumstances like darkness or bad weather because it is regarded official after the completion of the second stage (approximately equivalent to the former criterion of 50% of the scheduled distance under the previous format). At the conclusion of each stage, there is a competition caution, during which drivers may choose to make a pit stop before the restart for the following stage. Each stage's optional pit stop puts teams at risk of losing track position if they make a sluggish stop or decide not to pit. Also, with two laps remaining in the stage, pit road is shut down as soon as the race leader crosses the start-finish line.

At the conclusion of the first and second stages, the top 10 drivers are given championship points, which are given on a scale from 10 to 1. Following the final stage, each race's overall winner is granted 40 points, and the other drivers are given points in decreasing order, starting at 35 for finishing second and down to 2 for 35th place and 1 for 36th through 40th. Each stage's victor also receives a "playoff point," with the overall victor taking home five. The Can-Am Duel qualifying races for the Daytona 500 were converted into points-paying events for the first time since 1971; the top ten finishers in each of the two races received points.

The 16 drivers with the most victories following the 26-race regular season will advance to the playoffs, with championship points serving as a tiebreaker (re-branded from the "Chase for the Championship"). The top 10 drivers in the standings will now receive additional playoff points. The regular-season champion will receive 15, second place will receive 10, and the remaining drivers will receive points in decreasing order of 8 to 1. A driver's championship points will be reset to 2000 and their banked playoff points will be added to this total if they are eligible for the postseason. The playoffs will still follow the current multi-round elimination structure, and all races other than the championship race will carry over playoff points.

DRIVERS THAT COMPETED IN THE 2017 NASCAR SEASON

- Jimmie Johnson - Hendrick Motorsports
- Kyle Busch - Joe Gibbs Racing
- Martin Truex Jr. - Furniture Row Racing
- Kevin Harvick - Stewart-Haas Racing
- Denny Hamlin - Joe Gibbs Racing
- Brad Keselowski - Team Penske
- Chase Elliott - Hendrick Motorsports
- Matt Kenseth - Joe Gibbs Racing
- Kyle Larson - Chip Ganassi Racing
- Ryan Blaney - Wood Brothers Racing
- Jamie McMurray - Chip Ganassi Racing
- Joey Logano - Team Penske
- Kurt Busch - Stewart-Haas Racing
- Ricky Stenhouse Jr. - Roush Fenway Racing
- Ryan Newman - Richard Childress Racing
- Austin Dillon - Richard Childress Racing
- Kasey Kahne - Hendrick Motorsports
- Clint Bowyer - Stewart-Haas Racing
- Erik Jones - Furniture Row Racing
- Trevor Bayne - Roush Fenway Racing
- Aric Almirola - Richard Petty Motorsports
- Paul Menard - Richard Childress Racing
- AJ Allmendinger - JTG Daugherty Racing
- Danica Patrick - Stewart-Haas Racing
- Chris Buescher - JTG Daugherty Racing
- Michael McDowell - Leavine Family Racing
- Ty Dillon - Germain Racing
- David Ragan - Front Row Motorsports
- Matt DiBenedetto - Go FAS Racing
- Corey LaJoie - BK Racing
- Cole Whitt - TriStar Motorsports
- Gray Gaulding - BK Racing
- Jeffrey Earnhardt - Circle Sport - The Motorsports Group
- Reed Sorenson - Premium Motorsports
- Derrike Cope - Premium Motorsports

- Boris Said - Go FAS Racing
- Alon Day - BK Racing
- Ray Black Jr. - Rick Ware Racing
- Joey Gase - BK Racing
- Cody Ware - Rick Ware Racing
- Stephen Leicht - BK Racing
- DJ Kennington - Gaunt Brothers Racing
- Ryan Sieg - BK Racing

WINNER OF THE 2017 SPRINT CUP SERIES CHAMPIONSHIP.

Martin Truex Jr. defeated Kyle Busch by.681 seconds at Homestead-Miami Speedway on Sunday to win the Ford Eco-Boost 400 and his first Monster Energy NASCAR Cup Series championship following a thrilling, stunning race that had spectators on their feet long after the checkered flag. Furniture Row Racing, based in Denver, Colorado, won for Truex, who also brought home the team's first championship. In the final circuits, he held off Kyle Busch's fierce push to secure his eighth victory of the year and a 1.5-mile oval record seventh victory. In his 12th full-time season in the Cup, Truex wins the championship.

Yet it wasn't an easy road for Truex to the title. After learning that his longtime partner Sherry Pollex had ovarian cancer in 2014, Truex was forced to put his racing career on hold in order to take care of her. Pollex had chemotherapy and surgery, but the cancer came back in 2015. Truex and Pollex persevered in the face of difficulties, and Truex returned to the track with a fresh outlook.

In 2017, Truex and his squad, driven by crew chief Cole Pearn, made a solid start, winning the Daytona 500 to kick off the season and adding victories at Kansas, Kentucky, Las Vegas, and other tracks. Truex's prowess on the track and Pearn's tactical decisions from the pit box, as well as a strong partnership with Joe Gibbs Racing, which gave Furniture Row Racing technical support, all contributed to the team's success.

Truex was the overwhelming favorite to win the championship as the playoffs drew near. He finished first in one of the first three playoff races and second in the other, giving him significant points lead going into the Homestead finale. Kyle Busch, Kevin Harvick, and Brad Keselowski were also in the race to compete for the championship, but Truex managed to keep his composure under pressure and come out on top to win the race and realize a long-held desire.

In addition to his outstanding season, Truex's championship triumph was a remarkable accomplishment given the difficulties he and Pollex had encountered off the track. "This one's for her, and it's for all the other individuals out there who have gone through bad times," Truex said in his victory speech, dedicating the victory to Pollex and to all those who had fought cancer. The triumph confirmed Truex's status as one of NASCAR's top drivers and Furniture Row Racing's standing as a premier team.

NASCAR Xfinity SERIES FOR 2017

The 2017 Monster Energy NASCAR Cup Series marks the 69th season of American professional stock car racing overall and the 46th Cup series season in contemporary times. The 59th running of the Daytona 500, the Can-Am Duel qualifying sessions, and the Advance Auto Parts Clash all served as season openers at Daytona International Speedway. The season came to a close with the Ford EcoBoost 400 at Homestead-Miami Speedway. William Byron, the third-place finisher in the Ford EcoBoost 300 on Saturday and the 2017 NASCAR Xfinity Series champion, had the best performance among the Championship 4 contenders in the final race of the year at Florida's Homestead-Miami Speedway.

Cole Custer achieved his first career victory by winning the season's 33rd race, although the playoff system eliminated him from title contention.

Byron had an outstanding first season with the Xfinity Series, earning four victories and 3,328 points. He finished in the top 10 in 22 of the 33 races that season, proving to be a dependable and skilled driver.

One of Byron's key contributions in 2017 was his ability to deliver powerful performances on a variety of unique songs. He excelled on both short tracks and superspeedways, and he was able to remain competitive under trying conditions.

Byron received assistance from a skilled and knowledgeable crew, led by crew chief David Elenz and team owner Dale Earnhardt Jr. Elenz offered Byron suggestions for enhancing his driving skills and made wise decisions that helped him to stay competitive throughout the season.

In addition to his outstanding performance on the track, Byron showed extraordinary maturity and professionalism for a driver of his age. He maintained his commitment and engagement throughout the entire season, always seeking for ways to improve and use the lessons he had learned.

Byron's victory in the 2017 Xfinity Series Championship was proof of his skill, diligence, and dedication. Furthermore, it was a sign of larger things to come because he went on to have a fruitful NASCAR Cup Series career that included multiple race wins and a playoff spot.

The magnificent performance by William Byron will go down in history as one of the most memorable moments in the history of the series. The 2017 Xfinity Series Championship was a thrilling and memorable season overall.

OVERVIEW OF THE NASCAR 2018 SEASON

The 2018 Monster Energy NASCAR Cup Series is the 47th Cup series season in the modern era and the 70th season of NASCAR professional stock car racing in the United States. The Advance Auto Parts Clash, the Can-Am Duel qualifying events, and the 60th running of the Daytona 500 marked the start of the season at Daytona International Speedway. On September 9, 2018, the Brickyard 400 marked the conclusion of the regular season. On November 18, 2018, the Ford EcoBoost 400 at Homestead-Miami Speedway marked the conclusion of the playoffs.

The Chevrolet Camaro ZL1 made its début during this season, replacing the Chevrolet SS, and becoming the company's first coupe-based stock vehicle since the Monte Carlo SS was phased out in 2017. This was also the final year for BK Racing, which sold its equipment to Front Row Motorsports, and Furniture Row Racing, which ceased operations after 2018. Kasey Kahne also announced his intention to retire from racing at the end of the season but was forced to quit early in October 2018 after his health prevented him from doing so. Ford discontinued the Fusion after this season, and the Ford Mustang took its place in 2019.

The 2018 Daytona 500 was Danica Patrick's final NASCAR race, but it ended after the 102nd lap when she was engaged in a multicar accident. For Partrick, who had seven top-10 finishes during his stock car career, that was certainly not the way he wanted to retire.

A fresh batch of outstanding young drivers, including William Byron, Bubba Wallace, and Christopher Bell, debuted for the 2018 season. Byron made his Cup Series debut with Hendrick Motorsports after previously winning the Xfinity Series championship. Wallace made his Cup Series debut with Richard Petty Motorsports after competing in the Xfinity Series and the Camping World Truck Series. Bell, who had won the Truck Series title, raced for Joe Gibbs Racing in the Xfinity Series.

With four drivers vying for the championship going into the last race of the season, Joey Logano, Martin Truex Jr., Kevin Harvick, and Kyle Busch, the 2018 Cup Series championship race was one of the most intense in recent memory. Logano ultimately prevailed, taking home his first Cup Series victory.

Big events, including some memorable finishes, occurred throughout the 2018 season. In the final circuits of the autumn race at Martinsville Speedway, Joey Logano and Martin Truex Jr. engaged in one of the season's most memorable moments. On the last lap, Logano made contact with Truex Jr., sending him spinning and giving Logano the victory. In the final circuits of the spring race at Bristol Motor Speedway, Kyle Busch and Kyle Larson engaged in a side-by-side battle for the lead. Nonetheless, Busch prevailed, winning his second race of the year.

Following an examination of the rule's impact in 2017, as well as to take into consideration the decrease in pit crew workers, it was revealed in February 2018 that the vehicle damage policy put into place in 2017 had been changed. The repair window has been lengthened to six minutes, and the punishment for having an excessive number of crew members working on the vehicle has been changed from disqualification to a two-lap fine. Also, the first qualifying session on intermediate and short tracks has been shortened from 20 to 15 minutes.

Teams no longer need to start the race on the tires they used in qualifying, according to NASCAR's announcement on May 16, 2018, as teams that don't pass the inspection before qualifying gain an edge.

The use of the new "composite body" on the Cup Series vehicles during the 2018 season was not without controversy. The composite body, which debuted in 2018, is comprised of a combination of carbon fiber and resin and is intended to outperform the earlier steel bodies in terms of cost and durability. Several teams, however, claimed that other teams had manipulated the bodies to their advantage.

List Of Drivers Who Competed In The 2018 NASCAR Cup Series Season:

- Jamie McMurray - Chip Ganassi Racing
- Kyle Larson - Chip Ganassi Racing
- Chase Elliott - Hendrick Motorsports
- Jimmie Johnson - Hendrick Motorsports
- William Byron - Hendrick Motorsports
- Alex Bowman - Hendrick Motorsports
- Denny Hamlin - Joe Gibbs Racing
- Kyle Busch - Joe Gibbs Racing
- Daniel Suarez - Joe Gibbs Racing
- Erik Jones - Joe Gibbs Racing
- Matt Kenseth - Roush Fenway Racing
- Ricky Stenhouse Jr. - Roush Fenway Racing
- Trevor Bayne - Roush Fenway Racing
- Aric Almirola - Stewart-Haas Racing
- Kevin Harvick - Stewart-Haas Racing
- Kurt Busch - Stewart-Haas Racing
- Clint Bowyer - Stewart-Haas Racing
- Austin Dillon - Richard Childress Racing
- Ryan Newman - Richard Childress Racing
- Darrell Wallace Jr. - Richard Petty Motorsports
- AJ Allmendinger - JTG Daugherty Racing
- Chris Buescher - JTG Daugherty Racing
- Michael McDowell - Front Row Motorsports
- David Ragan - Front Row Motorsports
- Ty Dillon - Germain Racing
- Kasey Kahne - Leavine Family Racing

- Gray Gaulding - BK Racing
- Corey LaJoie - TriStar Motorsports
- Jeffrey Earnhardt - StarCom Racing
- Ross Chastain - Premium Motorsports
- BJ McLeod - Rick Ware Racing
- Matt DiBenedetto - Go Fas Racing
- Martin Truex Jr. - Furniture Row Racing
- Joey Logano - Team Penske
- Brad Keselowski - Team Penske
- Ryan Blaney - Team Penske
- Paul Menard - Wood Brothers Racing
- Brendan Gaughan - Beard Motorsports
- DJ Kennington - Gaunt Brothers Racing
- Timmy Hill - MBM Motorsports
- Blake Jones - BK Racing
- Justin Marks - Rick Ware Racing
- Landon Cassill - StarCom Racing
- Harrison Rhodes - Rick Ware Racing
- Kyle Weatherman - StarCom Racing

WINNER OF THE 2018 SPRINT CUP SERIES CHAMPIONSHIP.

Joseph Thomas Logano is a professional stock car racer from the United States. He was born on May 24, 1990. He participates in the NASCAR Cup Series on a full-time basis, driving the No. 22 Ford Mustang for Team Penske. The 2018 NASCAR Cup Series champion is Logano.

It was a competitive NASCAR Cup Series season in 2018, with several drivers taking victories and vying for the title throughout the year.

Joseph Thomas Logano is a professional stock car racer from the United States. He was born on May 24, 1990. After defeating Martin Truex Jr., Kevin Harvick, and Kyle Busch in a 1-2-3-4 finish for the "Championship 4" during the final round at Homestead, Joey Logano, driving for Team Penske in a Ford, won the championship. In addition to winning the spring race at Talladega and the fall event at Martinsville, Logano won three races throughout the season. The winner of the Daytona 500 was Austin Dillon.

As a 6-year-old quarter-midget racer from Connecticut, Logano started his racing career in 1996. He won the Jr. Stock Car Division of the Eastern Grand National Championship for the first time in 1997. He then won the Jr. Honda Division Championship in 1998, and the Lt. Mod. Division Championship in the early part of 1999. Later in 1999, Logano triumphed in the Sr. Stock, Lt. Mod, and Lt. B divisions, taking home three New England Regional Championships.

Logano was able to compete in the series thanks to a 2007 change in NASCAR regulations that enabled drivers older than 16 to race in the Grand National Division. After 13 starts in the Camping World East Series, he finished the 2007 Grand National season with five victories, three pole positions, ten Top 5 finishes, and ten Top 10 finishes. He also took home the championship with victories at Greenville-Pickens Speedway, Iowa Speedway, two wins at New Hampshire International Speedway, and Adirondack International Speedway. He has also raced in the NASCAR West Series once, finishing first in the No. 10 Joe Gibbs Racing Toyota after starting second at Phoenix International Raceway. Logano led 87 laps and defeated Peyton Sellers to win the Toyota All-Star Showdown at Irwindale Raceway on October 20, 2007.

Logano had a solid season in the 2018 NASCAR Cup Series, placing in the top 10 in 26 of the 36 races. He also finished in the top five 13 times, and his 934 laps led were the fourth-most of any driver in the series. Logano's victory in the season finale marked his 21st career Cup Series victory and second victory at Homestead-Miami Speedway.

Given that he had placed second in the Cup Series championship twice before, in 2014 and 2016, Logano's victory was a sort of redemption. Logano and his team, Team Penske, had a successful season in 2018, and Logano's crew chief, Todd Gordon, made tactical decisions that helped Logano position himself to win races.

Logano's triumph in the championship also gave Team Penske its second Cup Series victory; Brad Keselowski had won the title with them in 2012. Shell-Pennzoil, who had been Logano's primary sponsor since 2011, also won the championship for the first time.

2018 NASCAR Xfinity SERIES CHAMPIONSHIP

Tyler George Reddick is an American stock car racing driver who was born on January 11, 1996. He races in the NASCAR Cup Series full-time for 23XI Racing in the No. 45 Toyota Camry and the NASCAR Xfinity Series part-time for Sam Hunt Racing in the No. 24 Toyota Supra.

At the age of four, Reddick started racing in Outlaw Karts. Soon after, he moved on to mini sprints, midgets, dirt late models, and sprint cars. He was the youngest driver to win the East Bay Winter Nationals, qualify for the pole position at the Eldora Speedway World 100, and compete in the Lucas Oil Late Model Dirt Series. In World of Outlaws sprint car racing, he also holds the record for being the youngest driver to ever qualify for a feature race.

Reddick made his ARCA Racing Series debut in 2012, and at Rockingham Raceway in October of that same year, he won his first professional start in the NASCAR K&N Pro Series East.

The driver of the No. 9 JR Motorsports Chevrolet brought a remarkable season to a fitting close by winning the Ford EcoBoost 300 at Homestead-Miami Speedway and winning the 2018 NASCAR Xfinity Series championship.

In his first race driving the #9 Chevy, Reddick won the race at Daytona International Speedway to kick off the 2018 season, but he hasn't won a race since. Yet, despite having a very inconsistent regular season, he was still able to go on based on his point total from the round of 12 to the round of 8, then from the round of 8 to the Championship 4, which allowed him to win the title in the season's last game.

Reddick finished in the top nine of six of the seven playoff races, three of them in the top five, while his lowest position was 14th in the contest at Dover International Speedway. His average finish in these races was 6.29, compared to his 12.88 and 14.65 average finishes in the 33-race regular season and the 26-race postseason, respectively.

Reddick was also named the Sunoco Rookie of the Year for the 2018 NASCAR Xfinity Series.

The victory marks JR Motorsports' third driver championship in the past five years and second in a row. The group also triumphed in 2014 and 2017 thanks to Chase Elliott and William Byron.

Logano overtook Martin Truex Jr. with 12 laps remaining to win in Homestead and claim the 2018 Monster Energy NASCAR Cup Series championship.

Chevrolet won the NASCAR Xfinity Series Manufacturer Championship for 2018 thanks to its 15 victories.

OVERVIEW OF THE NASCAR 2019 SEASON

The 2019 NASCAR Cup Series, also known as the 2019 Monster Energy NASCAR Cup Series, was the 48th Cup series season in the current era and the 71st season of NASCAR professional stock car racing in the United States. The Advance Auto Parts Clash, the Gander RV Duel qualifying events, and the 61st edition of the Daytona 500 marked the start of the season at Daytona International Speedway. The Brickyard 400 in September marked the end of the regular season. On November 17, 2019, the Ford EcoBoost 400 at Homestead-Miami Speedway marked the conclusion of the playoffs.

After twelve years of continuous full-time Cup Series competition, drivers David Ragan and Paul Menard retired following the 2019 season. Inadvertently, it was the last time Chicagoland Racetrack was featured. The track was removed from the calendar for 2021 after the COVID-19 outbreak forced the cancellation of its event in 2020.

Although NASCAR chose a new tiered sponsorship structure over an extension offer from the energy drink business, this was Monster Energy's final season as the title sponsor. Busch Beer took over as the Cup series' title sponsor from Monster Energy.

Kyle Busch of Joe Gibbs Racing won the 2019 Bojangles' Southern 500 at Darlington Raceway to secure his second consecutive Regular Season Championship.

After winning the season finale at Homestead, Busch went on to win the championship. After being sidelined for the first 11 races of the 2015 season due to injury, it was his second title and the first one he had won after taking part in all 36 races of the season. Busch started the season with four victories in the first 14 races, but then he lost his next 21 races. The 2018 champion Logano lost out to him in the Round of 8 due to his early-season performance, which also gave him a ton of playoff points.

All of the other Championship 4 participants earned their spots through victories in the semifinal round. Among the title challengers at Homestead, those were Martin Truex Jr., Kevin Harvick, and Denny Hamlin, finishing in that order. In the 2018 championship race, Truex and Harvick came in second and third, respectively. Logano, the defending champion, came in fifth overall. Hamlin won the Daytona 500 even though he came up short in the championship. Three of the four title candidates belonged to Joe Gibbs Racing and Toyota, which also took 19 of the 36 races. While Daniel Hemric was named Rookie of the Year, Alex Bowman and Justin Haley each won for the first time in their professional careers. With 15 consecutive appearances in the Playoffs, seven-time Series Champion Jimmie Johnson would miss them for the first time since they began in 2004.

After twelve years of continuous full-time Cup Series competition, drivers David Ragan and Paul Menard retired following the 2019 season. Inadvertently, it was the last time Chicagoland Racetrack was featured. The track was removed from the calendar for 2021 after the COVID-19 outbreak forced the cancellation of its event in 2020.

An exciting championship race at Homestead-Miami Speedway capped off a good season for the 2019 NASCAR Cup Series overall. The season featured fierce competition and interesting races throughout.

List of drivers who competed in the 2018 NASCAR Cup Series season:

- Kurt Busch - Chip Ganassi Racing
- Kyle Larson - Chip Ganassi Racing
- Chase Elliott - Hendrick Motorsports
- Jimmie Johnson - Hendrick Motorsports
- Alex Bowman - Hendrick Motorsports
- William Byron - Hendrick Motorsports
- Martin Truex Jr. - Joe Gibbs Racing
- Kyle Busch - Joe Gibbs Racing
- Denny Hamlin - Joe Gibbs Racing
- Erik Jones - Joe Gibbs Racing
- Ryan Newman - Roush Fenway Racing
- Ricky Stenhouse Jr. - Roush Fenway Racing
- Chris Buescher - Roush Fenway Racing
- Kevin Harvick - Stewart-Haas Racing
- Aric Almirola - Stewart-Haas Racing
- Clint Bowyer - Stewart-Haas Racing
- Daniel Suarez - Stewart-Haas Racing
- Brad Keselowski - Team Penske
- Joey Logano - Team Penske
- Ryan Blaney - Team Penske
- Austin Dillon - Richard Childress Racing
- Tyler Reddick - Richard Childress Racing
- Daniel Hemric - Richard Childress Racing
- Bubba Wallace - Richard Petty Motorsports
- Ryan Preece - JTG Daugherty Racing
- AJ Allmendinger - Kaulig Racing
- Matt Tifft - Front Row Motorsports
- Michael McDowell - Front Row Motorsports
- David Ragan - Front Row Motorsports
- Ty Dillon - Germain Racing
- Matt DiBenedetto - Leavine Family Racing
- Corey LaJoie - Go Fas Racing
- Ross Chastain - Premium Motorsports
- Landon Cassill - StarCom Racing

- JJ Yeley - Premium Motorsports
- Quin Houff - Spire Motorsports
- Reed Sorenson - Premium Motorsports
- Brendan Gaughan - Beard Motorsports
- Joey Gase - MBM Motorsports
- Cody Ware - Rick Ware Racing
- Timmy Hill - MBM Motorsports
- Josh Bilicki - Rick Ware Racing

WINNER OF THE 2019 SPRINT CUP SERIES CHAMPIONSHIP.

Kyle Busch of Joe Gibbs Racing won the Ford EcoBoost 400, the 36th and final race of the season, at Homestead-Miami Speedway, clinching the 2019 NASCAR Cup Series title.

With his #18 Toyota and after having led a race-high 120 laps, Busch started this 267-lap Championship 4 season finale over the four-turn, 1.5-mile (2.414-kilometer) Homestead-Miami Speedway oval in Homestead, Florida. Martin Truex Jr., a teammate and title competitor, finished second in his #19 Toyota, and he won it by 4.578 seconds.

To win his second championship, Busch only had to finish ahead of Truex, teammate Denny Hamlin, and Kevin Harvick of Stewart-Haas Racing in the Championship 4.

After Jimmie Johnson, a seven-time champion, won his second championship in the 2007 campaign, he has became the first driver to do so. He also holds the distinction of being the first driver since the Championship 4 era's start in the 2014 season to win two championships.

While Truex won the championship in 2017, Harvick won it in 2014. Hamlin has yet to win his first championship.

Busch began the season finale on a winless streak of 21 races after failing to triumph at Pocono Raceway in early June. The other three drivers, meanwhile, each secured a spot in the Championship 4 by winning one of the three races in the round of 8. In the end, Harvick placed fourth in the season finale in his #4 Ford, while Hamlin placed tenth in his #11 Toyota.

Other than Busch, all three of the Championship 4 drivers had opportunities to win the race. Early on, Harvick claimed the lead and dominated the short runs. He found it problematic that there were only three caution flag periods in the race, just one of which was due to an accident on the circuit.

Early on in the race, Truex dominated, taking the lead on 98 of the first 120 circuits. He had to make an unplanned pit stop, though, since his pit team switched the tires on his left and right sides. Except from the five laps, he spent out in front of the leaders later in the race, when he did get back onto the lead lap, he never made it back to the front.

On the third and final stage of the race, Hamlin took the lead. But, when his team covered his grill with a large piece of tape, too much water leaked out of his #11 Toyota, forcing him to make an emergency pit stop to keep it from overheating and blowing up.

2019 NASCAR Xfinity SERIES RACE WINNERS

Tyler Reddick of Richard Childress Racing won the Ford EcoBoost 300, the season's 33rd and final race, at Homestead-Miami Speedway to claim the 2019 NASCAR Xfinity Series championship.

Reddick's championship was his second in two seasons as a full-time Xfinity Series driver after he had won the title last year with two victories while racing for JR Motorsports. This victory was his sixth of the year and the ninth of his career. Reddick is the only driver in the history of the Xfinity Series to win titles while competing for two separate teams.

Reddick won this 200-lap Championship 4 season finale by 1.038 seconds over Stewart-Haas Racing's Cole Custer, who finished in second place in his #00 Ford, after leading 84 laps over the four-turn, 1.5-mile (2.414-kilometer) Homestead-Miami Speedway track in Homestead, Florida.

To win his second straight championship, the 23-year-old native of Corning, California, only had to finish ahead of the other three Championship 4 contenders in this event. Winning took care of that, just like it did last year.

Justin Allgaier of JR Motorsports, Christopher Bell of Joe Gibbs Racing, and Custer made up the other three members of the Championship 4. In the Final 4 from the previous year, Reddick also defeated Custer and Bell.

With a second-place finish in this race, Custer, who won the 2017 season finale as a non-Championship 4 driver, finished behind Reddick in the championship standings, same as last year. Bell finished third in the standings with a fifth-place finish after coming in fourth previous season with an 11th-place showing in the season finale.

Allgaier had to settle for a 14th-place finish after a late flat tire forced him out of the top seven late in the race. He was the only member of the Championship 4 to not have led a lap during the competition. Custer led 15 laps, Bell led 37 lap, and Reddick led 84 lap

OVERVIEW OF THE NASCAR 2020 SEASON

The 2020 NASCAR Cup Series is the 49th season of the Cup Series' modern era and the 72nd season of NASCAR's professional stock car racing in the United States. The Busch Clash, the Bluegreen Vacations Duel qualifying events, and the 62nd edition of the Daytona 500 marked the start of the season at Daytona International Speedway. On August 29, the Coke Zero Sugar 400 at Daytona marked the end of the regular season. The Season Finale 500, the first finale at Phoenix Raceway on November 8, marked the end of the NASCAR playoffs.

After turning down Monster Energy's request to renew its title sponsorship, NASCAR adopted a new tiered sponsorship structure for this season. Busch Beer, Coca-Cola, GEICO, and Xfinity were named as the Premier Partners of the NASCAR Cup Series on December 5, 2019, taking the place of Monster Energy as the series' single title sponsor.

The Gen-6 car was supposed to be phased out after this season, with the Next Gen car (formerly the Gen-7 car) making its début in 2021.

The COVID-19 pandemic, however, delayed all NASCAR racing (and, consequently, testing) until the month of May, prompting the sanctioning organization to announce that the car's debut would be delayed by a year to 2022.

Jimmie Johnson, a seven-time series champion, Clint Bowyer, and Brendan Gaughan, a part-time driver, will all retire after the 2020 season, it was confirmed.

David Ragan, who resigned from full-time NASCAR competition after 2019, made a brief comeback this season to compete in the Daytona 500 in the Cup Series and a few Truck Series races for Rick Ware Racing, a team he cofounded with Front Row Motorsports (driving for DGR-Crosley). Additionally, 2020 marked the final year for Leavine Family Racing, owned by Bob Leavine's family, and Germain Racing, whose longtime sponsor GEICO announced they would part ways with the team at the end of the season. Bob Leavine's team had enough financial issues due to the COVID-19 pandemic that he had to close the team and sell its assets. On August 4, a purchaser was located.

Drivers from every NASCAR series, including nearly all of the Cup Series drivers, took part in the first eNASCAR iRacing Pro Invitational Series when the season was postponed due to the coronavirus.

List Of Drivers And Teams That Competed In The 2020 NASCAR Cup Series Season:

1. Kurt Busch – Chip Ganassi Racing
2. Kyle Larson - Chip Ganassi Racing
3. Ross Chastain - Chip Ganassi Racing (substitute driver for Larson after suspension)
4. Chase Elliott - Hendrick Motorsports
5. Jimmie Johnson - Hendrick Motorsports
6. Alex Bowman - Hendrick Motorsports

7. William Byron - Hendrick Motorsports
8. Martin Truex Jr. - Joe Gibbs Racing
9. Kyle Busch - Joe Gibbs Racing
10. Denny Hamlin - Joe Gibbs Racing
11. Erik Jones - Joe Gibbs Racing
12. Christopher Bell - Leavine Family Racing (now with Joe Gibbs Racing)
13. Bubba Wallace - Richard Petty Motorsports
14. Ryan Newman - Roush Fenway Racing
15. Chris Buescher - Roush Fenway Racing
16. Ricky Stenhouse Jr. - JTG Daugherty Racing (now with Trackhouse Racing Team)
17. Ryan Preece - JTG Daugherty Racing
18. Ty Dillon - Germain Racing
19. Matt Kenseth - Chip Ganassi Racing (substitute driver for Larson after suspension)
20. Kevin Harvick - Stewart-Haas Racing
21. Aric Almirola - Stewart-Haas Racing
22. Clint Bowyer - Stewart-Haas Racing
23. Cole Custer - Stewart-Haas Racing
24. Brad Keselowski - Team Penske
25. Joey Logano - Team Penske
26. Ryan Blaney - Team Penske
27. Austin Dillon - Richard Childress Racing
28. Tyler Reddick - Richard Childress Racing
29. Daniel Suarez - Gaunt Brothers Racing
30. John Hunter Nemechek - Front Row Motorsports
31. Michael McDowell - Front Row Motorsports
32. Matt DiBenedetto - Wood Brothers Racing
33. Corey LaJoie - Go Fas Racing
34. Brennan Poole - Premium Motorsports
35. Reed Sorenson - Premium Motorsports
36. Quin Houff - StarCom Racing
37. JJ Yeley - Rick Ware Racing
38. James Davison - Rick Ware Racing
39. Josh Bilicki - Rick Ware Racing
40. Timmy Hill - MBM Motorsports
41. Joey Gase - Tommy Baldwin Racing (part-time)
42. Chad Finchum - MBM Motorsports (part-time)

WINNER OF THE 2020 SPRINT CUP SERIES CHAMPIONSHIP.

William Clyde "Chase" Elliott II, a professional stock car racer from the United States, was born on November 28, 1995. He drives the No. 9 Chevrolet Camaro ZL1 for Hendrick Motorsports full-time in the NASCAR Cup Series, and the No. 35 Chevrolet Silverado for McAnally-Hilgemann Racing part-time in the NASCAR Craftsman Truck Series. He became the youngest champion in the NASCAR Nationwide Series and the first rookie to win a national series championship after winning the 2014 season. He is the son of Bill Elliott, the 1988 Winston Cup Series champion; along with Lee and Richard Petty and Ned and Dale Jarrett, the Elliotts are the third father-son NASCAR champions in history.

Elliott was one of thirteen sportsmen, including future NBA 2nd overall pick Michael Kidd-Gilchrist and future world number one golfer Jordan Spieth, who were highlighted as potential stars in the July 13, 2009, Sports Illustrated issue. Elliott participated in 40 races across several series in 2010, winning twelve races overall and placing in the top ten 38 times. In his third racing season, he took home victories in the Blizzard Series, Miller Lite, and Gulf Coast championships, earning him the title of Georgia Asphalt Pro Late Model Series Rookie of the Year. He won the Winchester 400 to cap the campaign. In April 2011, Elliott was selected by Sports Illustrated as the high school athlete of the week. He participated in the Champion Racing Association during the year and won the National Super Late Model title for the division. He won the Snowball Derby later that year, just after turning sixteen, making him the race's youngest champion. He outran DJ Vanderley, who finished in second place, by a record-breaking 0.229 seconds. He won the Alan Turner Snowflake 100, the Snowball Derby's warm-up race, for the second time in three years in 2012.

Elliott won the All American 400 in November 2013, making history by becoming the first driver to triumph in each of the four biggest short-track races in the nation (the All American 400, the Snowball Derby, the World Crown 300, and the Winchester 400). Elliott appeared to have made racing history in December when he won both the Snowball Derby and the Snowflake 100 in the same weekend. However, a piece of tungsten that was against Derby rules was discovered in Elliott's car during the post-race inspection. As a result, Elliott was disqualified, and Erik Jones was given the victory. In 2015, Elliott won the Snowball Derby after the first-place finisher, Christopher Bell, was declared ineligible.

In 2016, Elliott made a full-time move to the Cup Series, where he won the 2016 NASCAR Sprint Cup Series Rookie of the Year award. Hendrick Motorsports' first Cup Series championship since 2016 came from him at Phoenix, Arizona, in 2020. Seven of his 18 Cup Series victories in the past have come on paved surfaces.

With 42 laps left in the 312-lap race, Elliott finally forced Logano to relinquish the lead. At the renowned one-mile desert oval on the day, three of the four title candidates set lap records. While

Keselowski led 16 laps and Logano led 125, Elliott's 154 laps up front demonstrated his talent, drive, and the No. 9 Hendrick Motorsports Chevrolet team's readiness for this race. With a crucial victory at Martinsville (Va.) Speedway, he was only able to secure his spot in the four-driver championship field, and he made the most of it on Sunday.

After failing pre-race inspection twice, Elliott was forced to start last in the Season Finale 500. Despite this, Elliott eventually led a race-high 153 laps to win the race and the championship. He achieved the second-youngest driver to win a Cup championship at the age of 24.

NASCAR XFINITY SERIES SEASON WINNER

Austin Louis Cindric, an American professional race car driver, was born on September 2, 1998. He drives the No. 2 Ford Mustang for Team Penske in the NASCAR Cup Series full-time.

In North Carolina, Cindric began his racing career in semi-pro Legends cars and Bandolero events. He competed in the U.S. F2000 National Championship in 2013 and 2014 after enrolling in the Skip Barber Racing School to get experience in road racing. With a best finish of seventh in the season finale, he drove for Andretti Autosport in 2013 and came in 17th in the points standings. He changed teams to Pabst Racing Services in 2014, finishing 14th in the standings with a podium result in second place on the oval at Lucas Oil Raceway. He participated in and won a race in historic sportscar racing in a Porsche 944.

Cindric started racing in the World RallyCross Championship Lites in 2014, and at the X Games Austin that year, he won the bronze medal. He raced with Racers Edge Motorsports in the IMSA Continental Tire Sports Car Challenge for the first time in October at Road Atlanta, finishing 17th with co-driver David Levine. He was accepted into the Porsche North American Junior Academy during the year. Cindric raced the No. 63 Mercedes-Benz SLS AMG for Erebus Motorsport in the 2015 Bathurst 12 Hour at the age of 17, making him the event's youngest competitor. Cindric finished 21st overall and eighth in his class. In 2015, he started taking part in the CTSCC on a regular basis, driving for Multimatic Motorsports with co-driver Jade Buford. He became the youngest (age 17) winner in the series when he took first place in the CTSCC event at Canadian Tire Motorsport Park in July.

He participated in the Pirelli World Challenge in 2016 as K-PAX Racing's No. 6 McLaren driver.

Moreover, Cindric led 947 laps in the No. 22 Ford, a career high, and won 11 stage races in 2020. Being the first Team Penske driver to win the championship under the new series scoring structure, the teenage driver earned the NXS regular season championship. Cindric made it into the NXS Championship 4 at Phoenix Raceway with a steady and successful playoff run.

Cindric won Stage 2 of the championship race and led 72 laps overall in his 100th Xfinity Series appearance. After a crucial finish to the race in which Wilson requested new tires during a last-minute pit stop, Cindric and the No. 22 team won the championship. This was his first Xfinity Series championship and the eighth series victory of his career.

OVERVIEW OF THE NASCAR 2021 SEASON

The 2021 NASCAR Cup Series marked the 50th season of the contemporary Cup Series and the 73rd season of NASCAR professional stock car racing in the United States. The Busch Clash, non-points race that opened the season at Daytona International Speedway, was raced on the road course instead of the oval for the first time ever. The Bluegreen Vacations Duel qualification races and the 63rd running of the Daytona 500, the first points race of the year, were held after that race. The 2021 Coke Zero Sugar 400, which took place on August 28 at Daytona, served as the final race of the regular season, and Kyle Larson emerged victorious. On October 31, 2021, Chevy won the Xfinity 500 at Martinsville Speedway, earning its 40th Manufacturer's Championship and first since 2015. On November 7, the NASCAR Cup Series Championship Race at Phoenix Raceway brought a conclusion to the postseason, with Larson winning his first Cup Series title after a 10-win campaign.

The Next Gen car, which featured modern technology and design aspects intended at enhancing safety and competitiveness, was introduced for the 2021 season, among other upgrades. The season also saw the installation of a new schedule, with numerous tracks being added and deleted from the previous year's schedule, as well as the continuation of the playoff system, which was initially established in 2004.

High levels of competition were present throughout the 2021 season, with numerous drivers competing for the championship and winning events. Kyle Larson, who won a career-high 10 races during the season and rejoined NASCAR after serving a suspension for using a racial epithet in a virtual race in 2020, won the championship. One of the most significant races on the program, the Coca-Cola 600, was won by Larson as part of his dominance.

Denny Hamlin, who won seven races and was second in the standings, and Martin Truex Jr., who won three races and took third place, were two other significant drivers during the season. The incumbent Cup Series champion, Chase Elliott, won five races and came in fifth overall.

The season was notable for the retirement of a number of seasoned drivers, including Matt Kenseth and Jimmie Johnson, who hung up their racing boots following the 2021 Daytona 500 and 2020 season, respectively.

The COVID-19 pandemic's ongoing effects on racing as well as the emergence of new ownership groups, including Michael Jordan and Denny Hamlin's 23XI Racing squad, were among off-track changes that the 2021 season was notable for.

Overall, the 2021 NASCAR Cup Series had a good season because to fierce racing, thrilling races, and important upgrades meant to enhance fan satisfaction, safety, and competition. Throughout the 2022 season, the Next Gen car will continue to be used, with the goal of significantly enhancing the sport for all parties involved—drivers, teams, and spectators.

A total of 23 teams participated in the 2021 NASCAR Cup Series, which featured competition in a number of events throughout the year.

The Teams Who Participated In The 2021 Season Are Listed Below:

- Kurt Busch - Chip Ganassi Racing
- Brad Keselowski - Team Penske
- Austin Dillon - Richard Childress Racing
- Kevin Harvick - Stewart-Haas Racing
- Kyle Busch - Joe Gibbs Racing
- Ryan Newman - Roush Fenway Racing
- Tyler Reddick - Richard Childress Racing
- Chase Elliott - Hendrick Motorsports
- Denny Hamlin - Joe Gibbs Racing
- Chris Buescher - Roush Fenway Racing
- Matt DiBenedetto - Wood Brothers Racing
- Ryan Blaney - Team Penske
- Kyle Larson - Hendrick Motorsports
- Christopher Bell - Joe Gibbs Racing
- Ricky Stenhouse Jr. - JTG Daugherty Racing
- Joey Logano - Team Penske
- William Byron - Hendrick Motorsports
- Michael McDowell - Front Row Motorsports
- Aric Almirola - Stewart-Haas Racing
- Alex Bowman - Hendrick Motorsports
- Bubba Wallace - 23XI Racing
- Ryan Preece - JTG Daugherty Racing
- Daniel Suárez - Trackhouse Racing Team
- Cole Custer - Stewart-Haas Racing
- Erik Jones - Richard Petty Motorsports
- Ross Chastain - Chip Ganassi Racing
- Anthony Alfredo - Front Row Motorsports
- Corey LaJoie - Spire Motorsports
- Quin Houff - StarCom Racing
- Cody Ware - Rick Ware Racing
- Josh Bilicki - Rick Ware Racing
- BJ McLeod - Live Fast Motorsports
- James Davison - Rick Ware Racing
- Garrett Smithley - Motorsports Business Management
- Timmy Hill - Motorsports Business Management

- Ty Dillon - Gaunt Brothers Racing
- David Starr - MBM Motorsports
- Joey Gase - Petty Ware Racing
- Chris Windom - Rick Ware Racing
- Derrike Cope - Rick Ware Racing

Throughout the course of the season, these teams ran a total of 23 cars, with each team normally running one. The season began on February 14, 2021, at the Daytona International Speedway, and ended on November 7, 2021, at the Phoenix Raceway. The drivers and teams participated in a total of 36 races.

WINNER OF THE 2021 SPRINT CUP SERIES CHAMPIONSHIP.

The 2021 NASCAR Cup Series season marked the 50th Cup series season in the modern era and the 73rd season of competitive stock car racing in the United States. A number of modifications were made during the season, including the debut of the Next Gen car and the reinstatement of practice and qualifying sessions following their cancellation in 2020 due to the COVID-19 epidemic.

Kyle Larson, who had an outstanding season and won his first championship, was the 2021 NASCAR Cup Series champion. Larson started his racing career in go-karts at the age of seven. He was born on July 31, 1992, in Elk Grove, California.

Before making his NASCAR debut in 2013, Larson advanced through the ranks of racing by competing in a number of dirt track competitions. After making a full-time entry into the Cup Series in 2014, he rapidly displayed his talent by taking first place in a Cup Series race in 2016.

But in 2020, Larson's career was put on hold when NASCAR banned him for using a racial slur during an iRacing competition. After receiving harsh criticism, Larson was fired from Chip Ganassi Racing, one of the best Cup Series teams.

Larson was reinstated in 2021 and signed with Hendrick Motorsports, one of the best teams in the Cup Series, following the completion of sensitivity training and a meeting with NASCAR officials. Larson had an outstanding season with Hendrick Motorsports, winning a series-high 10 races and setting the most lap records of any driver.

A sort of comeback narrative and redemption, Larson's strong performance in the 2021 season. In spite of the controversy and hardship he encountered in 2020, Larson was able to learn from his errors and accomplish his ultimate objective of winning a Cup Series championship.

Larson had a successful season with Hendrick Motorsports, and his crew chief, Cliff Daniels, made tactical choices that helped Larson position himself to win races. With Larson's victory, Hendrick Motorsports won their 14th Cup Series championship, tying Petty Enterprises for the most championships in NASCAR history.

With Larson's victory, Hendrick Motorsports won their 14th Cup Series championship, tying Petty Enterprises for the most championships in NASCAR history. With his victory in 2021, Larson confirmed both his position as one of the best Cup Series drivers and his spot in NASCAR history.

NASCAR XFINITY SERIES WINNER FOR THE SEASON

Daniel Hemric is an American stock car racing driver who was born on January 27, 1991. He is a full-time competitor in the NASCAR Xfinity Series, piloting Kaulig Racing's No. 11 Chevrolet Camaro.

Hemric started his career in short track racing before moving up to the NASCAR Camping World Truck Series, where he competed for Brad Keselowski Racing in 2015 and 2016. Prior to competing for Richard Childress Racing in the Monster Energy NASCAR Cup Series in 2019, he completed two full seasons in the NASCAR Xfinity Series, making it to the NASCAR playoffs in both seasons.

Despite holding a two-year deal with RCR, Hemric stated on August 17, 2019, that he was "doubtful" regarding his fate for 2020. Hemric would be released after the 2019 season, the team announced one month later on September 17. Hemric won his first Busch Pole Award of his career at the October Kansas race. In terms of total points, he placed 25th at the end of the year. Hemric took home the 2019 NASCAR Rookie of the Year award in spite of a lackluster debut campaign.

In 2020, Hemric made a comeback to the Xfinity Series, joining Dale Earnhardt Jr., Jeb Burton, and the No. 8 car of JR Motorsports for a 21-race season. Throughout the year, he had 12 top ten finishes.

Hemric returned to full-time competition when he switched to Joe Gibbs Racing's No. 18 Xfinity vehicle for the 2021 campaign. After an incident on the pit road during the Atlanta race, he got into a brawl with Noah Gragson at the finish line. NASCAR did not punish either driver. Hemric qualified for the Playoffs despite recording zero victories during the regular season in 2021 due to his reliability. Hemric will take over driving the No. 11 in 2022 from Justin Haley, who will go to Kaulig Racing's No. 31 in the Cup Series full-time, according to an announcement made on September 25 by Kaulig Racing.

Hemric would secure his spot in the Final 4 alongside Noah Gragson, A. J. Allmendinger, and Austin Cindric because of his dependability. Hemric won the first race of his NASCAR career and the 2021 Xfinity Series championship on November 6 at Phoenix Raceway thanks to a last-lap, overtime overtaking of Cindric. Prior to winning his first race, Hemric tied Dale Jarrett for the most runner-up finishes in the history of the Xfinity Series with ten.

OVERVIEW OF THE NASCAR 2022 SEASON

The 2022 NASCAR Cup Series is the 51st season of the current Cup Series and the 74th season of NASCAR professional stock car racing in the United States. The Busch Lite Clash at The Coliseum, which kicked off the season on February 6, took place in the Los Angeles Memorial Coliseum. The 64th running of the Daytona 500, the first points race of the season, took place at Daytona International Speedway on February 20, and it was followed by the qualifying rounds for the Bluegreen Vacations Duel on February 17. The Coke Zero Sugar 400, also held at Daytona, marked the end of the regular season on August 27. The Cook Out Southern 500 at Darlington Raceway on September 4 marked the start of the NASCAR playoffs, which concluded on November 6 with the NASCAR Cup Series Championship Race at Phoenix Raceway, where Joey Logano won his second Cup Series championship following a 4-win campaign. The Next Gen Automobile made its debut this season after being delayed owing to the COVID-19 pandemic from its scheduled 2021 release. Moreover, USA Network, which replaces the now-defunct NBCSN, is covering races for the first time this season.

Since Mars, Incorporated declared on December 20, 2021 that it would stop sponsoring NASCAR after the 2022 season, this will be its final year in that capacity. Since the 2008 season, they have served as the primary sponsor of Kyle Busch's No. 18 Joe Gibbs Racing car, mostly through the M&M's company. Before that, they supported the No. 36 MB2 Motorsports vehicle from 1997 to 2002 and the No. 38 Robert Yates Racing vehicle from 2003 to 2007. The JGR No. 18 is driven by Kyle Busch for the remainder of this campaign. Busch confirmed his departure from JGR for Richard Childress Racing in 2023 after months of contract negotiations with JGR and efforts to find a new sponsor for M&M's in 2023.

A streak of 62 years without a race winner being disqualified ended this season (which started in 1960). Denny Hamlin's victory in the race at Pocono Raceway was revoked because he failed the post-race inspection. (Thereafter, the victory was awarded to initial third-place finisher Chase Elliott since Hamlin's Joe Gibbs Racing teammate Kyle Busch had likewise failed post-race inspection and had been disqualified.) Since the rule was adopted in 2019 disqualifying the winner if their car failed post-race inspection, it has never occurred in a Cup Series race. Drivers from seven different nations competed in the event at Watkins Glen International, which was the most in series history.

Elliott of Hendrick Motorsports won the regular season title after the race at Watkins Glen. At Martinsville Speedway, Chevrolet won its 41st manufacturers' title prior to the 2022 Xfinity 500. [8] The award for NASCAR Rookie of the Year went to Team Penske's Austin Cindric.

This season's final race saw 19 different drivers claim victory, tying the record for the modern era (1972–present) set in 2001. Austin Cindric, Chase Briscoe, Ross Chastain, Daniel Suárez, and Tyler Reddick are the five drivers that each claimed their first career victory. The second races of their careers were won by Chastain, Reddick, Christopher Bell, Bubba Wallace, and Chris Buescher. Wallace and Buescher both achieved first-place finishes in non-weather-shortened races. The 2022 season was one of the most competitive in history thanks to victories by William Byron, Reddick, Bell, Austin Dillon, and Erik Jones in their third and fourth career races, respectively.

DRIVERS AND TEAMS IN THE NASCAR 2022 SEASON

DRIVERS	TEAMS
Aric Almirola	Stewart-Haas Racing
Christopher Bell	Joe Gibbs Racing
Josh Bilicki	Spire Motorsports
Ryan Blaney	Team Penske
Alex Bowman	Hendrick Motorsports
Chase Briscoe	Stewart-Haas Racing
Chris Buescher	RFK Racing
Harrison Burton	Wood Brothers Racing
Kyle Busch	Joe Gibbs Racing
Kurt Busch	23XI Racing
William Byron	Hendrick Motorsports
Ross Chastain	Trackhouse Racing Team
Austin Cindric	Team Penske
Cole Custer	Stewart-Haas Racing
Austin Dillon	Richard Childress Racing
Ty Dillon	Petty GMS Motorsports
Chase Elliott	Hendrick Motorsports
Todd Gilliland	Front Row Motorsports
Justin Haley	Kaulig Racing
Denny Hamlin	Joe Gibbs Racing
Kevin Harvick	Stewart-Haas Racing
Erik Jones	Petty GMS Motorsports
Brad Keselowski	RFK Racing
Corey LaJoie	Spire Motorsports
Kyle Larson	Hendrick Motorsports
Joey Logano	Team Penske
Michael McDowell	Front Row Motorsports
BJ McLeod	Live Fast Motorsports
Tyler Reddick	Richard Childress Racing
Ricky Stenhouse Jr.	JTG Daugherty Racing
Daniel Suarez	Trackhouse Racing Team
Martin Truex Jr.	Joe Gibbs Racing
Bubba Wallace	23XI Racing

WINNER OF THE 2022 SPRINT CUP SERIES CHAMPIONSHIP.

At the Phoenix Raceway in Avondale, Arizona, Joey Logano won the NASCAR Cup Series championship, taking the trophy home after 312 laps. Logano won the 2022 Busch Lite Clash at The Coliseum to kick off the 2022 racing season. At Darlington, he upset both William Byron and the audience by pushing Byron into the wall with two laps remaining to earn his first victory of the year. At the first Gateway race, Logano won for the second time in the current campaign. He won in Las Vegas during the playoffs to advance to the Final 4, then triumphed in Phoenix to capture his second Cup Series championship.

On the final miles, Logano and Chastain began to compete for the championship. Bell's delayed pit stop caused him to lose ground, and Elliott's car had been injured early in the race.

Roger Penske, the team owner, had a successful year thanks to Logano's triumph. For the first time ever, Team Penske won both titles in the same year thanks to Will Power's IndyCar victory.

NASCAR XFINITY CHAMPION FOR 2022

In 2022, Ty Gibbs' debut season generated a steady stream of news articles. With six victories coming into the Championship 4 finale at the age of just 20, Gibbs has been the Xfinity Series' standout driver—for better or worse.

Phoenix Raceway was where Gibbs' fame shone the brightest as he won the series in his first Xfinity season. In the championship race, the No. 54 Joe Gibbs Racing driver defeated Noah Gragson, Justin Allgaier, and Josh Berry of JR Motorsports.

At 20 years, 1 month, and 1 day old, Gibbs overtook current Cup Series veterans Chase Elliott and William Byron to become the fourth-youngest champion in series history. Elliott, who won the Xfinity championship in 2014 at the age of 18, is the youngest NASCAR National Series champion; Byron, who won the NXS championship in 2017, is the next-youngest.

During his ascent, Gibbs dominated the ARCA Menards Series, winning 18 races over the course of three seasons and collecting the checkered flag at an absurd percentage of 38.3% in 47 starts. He won all six of his combined outings in the West and East Series as well as 10 of the 20 races in the Menards Series, making him practically unbeatable in 2021 across all three ARCA banners.

The teen was invited up for a part-time position with his grandfather's JGR team after demonstrating complete command at the ARCA level. He took the wheel of the No. 54 Toyota and quickly established himself in the series where legends are born.

His Xfinity start for his first job? A thrilling victory for Gibbs, who was 18 at the time, on the road circuit at Daytona, leading 14 of the race's 56 laps.

While he wasn't championship eligible, Gibbs continued to flourish in 2021, winning three more races. The Xfinity contingency heard loud and plain that the quickly-rising potential was destined to be a title contender soon.

With the No. 45 23XI Racing Toyota, Gibbs finished in the top 20 three times in his first three Cup outings, including once at Michigan International Speedway, which was a career-high. Gibbs never achieved another similar result before the championship race, but he gained significant experience behind the wheel of the Next Gen vehicle and should be ready to make the full-time transition to the Cup level when the time comes.

Although his sixth victory in the penultimate race of 2022 at Martinsville Speedway was not without criticism, it solidified his place in the Championship 4 and has now led to the 20-year-first old's of what may be many titles to come.

With a possible promotion to the Cup Series on his grandfather's team, Gibbs will have a lot of eyes on him as he develops into a championship-caliber driver at the top level of the sport.